of his testimony. He lives what he writes! You will feel like you are sitting down having a heart-to-heart conversation with him as you open these pages and have your life transformed!"

Cindy Jacobs, Generals International

"Ché Ahn exudes the blessed life. He illustrates how to live in the blessing of the Lord. And this blessing touches every area of his life: family, ministry, health, finances, relationships and more. This is not a side issue. Without a proper theology of blessing, we will never be able to disciple nations according to the Great Commission. Ché brings life and freedom to a much-needed subject that affects every area of our lives. It comes from his personal relationship with Christ, which means he brings us this message with authority—authority to change every reader who prayerfully considers the truths presented in the book. Read, enjoy and be blessed! We owe it to the world around us that they might know what kind of heavenly Father we have."

Bill Johnson, Bethel Church; author, *Hosting the Presence*

GOD WANTS *to* BLESS YOU!

How *to* Experience the Unconditional Goodness of God

CHÉ AHN

Chosen

a division of Baker Publishing Group
Minneapolis, Minnesota

Published by Chosen Books
11400 Hampshire Avenue South
Bloomington, Minnesota 55438
www.chosenbooks.com

Chosen Books is a division of
Baker Publishing Group, Grand Rapids, Michigan

Printed in the United States of America

Library of Congress Cataloging-in-Publication Data

Ahn, Ché.
    God wants to bless you! : how to experience the unconditional goodness of God / Ché Ahn.
        pages cm
    Includes bibliographical references.
    Summary: "Pastor Ché Ahn reveals ten biblical blessings to proclaim in prayer that will unleash God's presence, purpose, and abundance in your life"—Provided by publisher.
        ISBN 978-0-8007-9773-7 (pbk. : alk. paper)
    1. Christian life. 2. God (Christianity)—Love. I. Title.
    BV4501.3.A3834 2015
    248.4—dc23   2015005497

Unless otherwise indicated, Scripture quotations are from the New King James Version. Copyright © 1982 by Thomas Nelson, Inc. Used by permission. All rights reserved.

Scripture quotations identified CEV are from the Contemporary English Version © 1991, 1992, 1995 by American Bible Society. Used by permission.

Scripture quotations identified ESV are from The Holy Bible, English Standard Version® (ESV®), copyright © 2001 by Crossway, a publishing ministry of Good News Publishers. Used by permission. All rights reserved. ESV Text Edition: 2007

Scripture quotations identified MESSAGE are from The Message by Eugene H. Peterson, copyright © 1993, 1994, 1995, 2000, 2001, 2002. Used by permission of NavPress Publishing Group. All rights reserved.

Scripture quotations identified NASB are from the New American Standard Bible®, copyright © 1960, 1962, 1963, 1968, 1971, 1972, 1973, 1975, 1977, 1995 by The Lockman Foundation. Used by permission.

Scripture quotations identified NIV are from the Holy Bible, New International Version®. NIV®. Copyright © 1973, 1978, 1984, 2011 by Biblica, Inc.™ Used by permission of Zondervan. All rights reserved worldwide. www.zondervan.com

Scripture quotations identified NLT are from the Holy Bible, New Living Translation, copyright © 1996, 2004, 2007 by Tyndale House Foundation. Used by permission of Tyndale House Publishers, Inc., Carol Stream, Illinois 60188. All rights reserved.

Scripture quotations identified NRSV are from the New Revised Standard Version of the Bible, copyright © 1989, by the Division of Christian Education of the National Council of the Churches of Christ in the United States of America. Used by permission. All rights reserved.

Scripture quotations identified KJV are from the King James Version of the Bible.

Cover design by Gearbox

To my beautiful bride
and best friend,
Sue Ahn

Contents

Acknowledgments

First, I want to thank my Lord Jesus for giving me the grace to write this book. All honor and glory truly goes to Him.

I want to thank my wonderful wife, Sue, and my children—Gabriel and Monica, Grace and Steve, Joy and Kuoching and Mary—for all their support as I feverishly worked on this book during our winter family vacation so that I could make the deadline. Thank you for sacrificing our vacation time together, although we had a great and memorable minivacation in San Diego.

Thanks also to the pastors, intercessors and members of HRock Church as they prayed for this book project and me.

Thank you, Jane Campbell of Chosen Books, for extending my deadline another month. Thank you for believing in this book project and me, and for being a good friend over the years.

Finally, I want to thank my three editors: Linda Radford, who helped me launch this book; Pastor David Oh, who helped me with three of the decrees; and Mark Miller, who made the final edits.

Introduction

How This Book Came to Be

God Wants to Bless You! is about living a blessed life, and it was birthed in my spirit in a unique way. In December 2013, while my family and I were on our winter vacation after Christmas, I received an unusual message on my cell phone. It was more of a short prophetic word of encouragement from my good friend Bob Hartley. Bob is a successful businessman in Kansas City with an extraordinary gift of prophecy. The message he left on my cell phone ended up bearing significant weight in my life and the ministry God has asked me to steward.

Bob told me that I was to decree ten scriptural blessings over my local church, HRock Church, and also over our network of churches, Harvest International Ministry (HIM). I got excited. I had been seeking God for the new message series that I would start in January, and I had been stuck on what to preach. When I heard the phone message, my spirit leapt—I knew Bob's message was from the Lord. I eagerly called him back.

"Thanks, Bob, for leaving the message on my voice mail. That is great—I am to declare ten scriptural blessings over my church starting in January. So . . . what decrees am I suppose to make?"

"I don't know," he replied. "I didn't get specifics from God. I just heard that you were to make the decrees. I think God wants you to seek Him about what they are."

I was a little disappointed, and I almost said, sarcastically, "Thanks a lot, Bob." But he was right. I knew God wanted me to seek Him about His blessing, a blessing that is real and alive in my life, and express it in such a way that would bless all who heard those decrees. Around this time, one of our HIM pastors, John Park, told me over dinner that he had given a message on the blessings of God and declared them over his congregation. It had been a tremendous blessing to his church. He e-mailed me his sermon notes.

After much prayer, I compiled ten decrees of blessing, first pronouncing them over my congregation at HRock Church in Pasadena. I was surprised by the response of our church members; many started to experience breakthrough in their lives. Increasingly, I am learning that a certain kind of power is released in a decree that is not present in merely a teaching about blessing. I believe that these decrees will change your life and that you, too, will receive significant breakthrough as you speak them over your life.

God's Nature Is to Bless

As I travel the world, I constantly meet Christians who understand that God does indeed bless them, but who show little evidence of that blessing in their lives. In honest and intimate conversation, many tell me that they have listened to many teachings about blessing, but they feel unworthy to be blessed. They may be struggling with some type of addiction, have had an affair, realize they have manipulated others for personal gain or failed to achieve some goal they deemed important. Whatever the reason, they judge themselves not good enough and feel guilty and ashamed.

Without realizing it, these souls have put conditions on God's blessings, turning the blessing into a payoff for good performance. They fail to understand the unconditional love of Abba God, who desires to bless them more than they desire to be blessed. They disqualify themselves from the blessings that He would freely give if only they would receive them by faith.

Their situation reminds me of a fable told by the late Dutch priest and author Henri Nouwen: There was a man who would meditate every morning under a tree close to a riverbank. One morning, as he finished meditating, he noticed a scorpion floating helplessly in the water, close to drowning. The man stood on the tree roots and stretched over the river to pick up the scorpion, but it stung his outstretched hand. Instinctively, he drew his hand back and winced. But, determined to assist the scorpion, he stretched over the river again to pull it out of the water. Once again the scorpion stung him, this time deeply penetrating his hand with its poisonous tail.

The man yelped in pain and drew back his hand, which was now swollen and bloody. At that moment, a passerby saw him and said, "Are you crazy? Only a fool would risk his life for the sake of an ugly, evil creature like that. Don't you know you could kill yourself trying to save that ungrateful scorpion?"

The man looked calmly at the passerby and gently said, "My friend, just because it is the scorpion's nature to sting, that does not change my nature to save."[1]

We must not confuse our actions with God's nature. Nothing we do or fail to do can change the fact that Abba God desires to bless us. It is His nature to do so. We can react with unbelief and push Him away because we do not feel worthy. We can hold on to negative thoughts. Like the scorpion we can remain helpless and struggle when He has supplied for our every need in abundance and longs for us to receive His supply.

Ephesians 1:3 tells us, "Blessed be the God and Father of our Lord Jesus Christ, who has blessed us with every spiritual blessing in the heavenly places in Christ." Every blessing in the heavenly realms God has already given to each believer, based on the greatest event in history: the death and resurrection of Jesus. But our job is to pull it down to earth by faith. This book is written to encourage believers to boldly step forward, decree God's blessing over themselves and others and learn to wear God's blessing well.

PART I

The Power of Blessing

1

The Blessing Hunger

When you walk into a jewelry store, you never see the diamonds displayed on a white backdrop. They always have a dark setup, usually black velvet. In order to really appreciate God's love and His heart to bless—the diamond—let me paint a dark framework of humanity's need and hunger for the Father's blessing.

A Fatherless Generation

The present young generation are losing their fathers. Some fathers disappear before their children are even born, their identity unknown. Other fathers are alienated through divorce and disappear over time. Still others are emotionally distant or unavailable due to preoccupation with careers or other personal interests. We live on an orphan planet.

Absent fathers leave their children with tremendous unmet needs that frequently lead to destructive consequences. Children often wind up looking in all the wrong places as they try to attain an inner sense of security and significance that only a father can provide. *The Fatherless Generation*, for example, reports that more than 70 percent of runaway children, pregnant teenagers, youth with behavioral disorders, high school dropouts and youth in prisons come from fatherless homes.[1]

The dilemma of fatherlessness was captured well in *The Breakfast Club*, one of the most popular teen films of all time. Though it was set in the mid-1980s, its principles are almost timeless. The movie follows five high school students from different social strata and their journey of self-discovery during nine hours of Saturday detention. Two are highly popular, the "social princess" and the "buff athletic jock." The others are on the outer fringes of school society, the "brainy nerd," the "basket case" and the rebellious, defiant "misfit."

At the start of their detention day, they regard each other with contempt and exchange verbal putdowns. It appears that they have nothing in common, but as time passes, they become increasingly self-disclosing as they engage in various activities. By the end, through transparent discussion, they discover that they all share a powerful need: to be accepted and validated by their parents, especially their fathers.

In compelling ways, this unmet need has shaped the personality and behavior of each student. The jock and brain are both trying to live up to their fathers' incessant demands to perform and feel increasingly doubtful of their ability. Both in their own ways find themselves unsure of their identities and caught up in behaviors to maintain their public images that leave them with self-contempt. The basket case has adopted aberrant behavior to attract the attention of her neglectful parents, while the misfit vents his anger toward his physically and emotionally abusive father in rebellion toward all authority figures. One can easily forecast a future mental hospital placement for the basket case and prison sentence for the misfit. The princess struggles with her privileged image that masks the reality of her parents' failing marriage and forces her into a role she experiences as self-alienating.

With their longing for parental validation unmet, all of them have embarked on a life journey to find some way to fulfill their inner restlessness, without success. Unless somehow resolved, this quest will likely continue to dominate the rest of their lives, whether they realize it or not.

Desire for affirmation from our fathers is a deep human need. Without it we wander in life, looking for ways to patch up the deficits it leaves. Those of us who have enjoyed the presence of a loving, involved father can count ourselves fortunate indeed. But as many benefits as the active, loving presence of a father brings, there is another, even deeper longing that we all experience but do not know how to satisfy. At some point, we experience a void within that we cannot fill.

We try to gratify our hunger with achievement, success, wealth, fame, attainment of "stuff," sexual exploits and on and on, but nothing satiates us. Everything we grasp in a bid for fulfillment turns to ashes. Everywhere we turn, the grass is greener than where we stand. The toys we buy, vacations we take or temporary relief we seek through drugs or alcohol do not keep us from waking up in the real world, with the incessant, unidentified longing still gnawing in our hearts. Sometimes this longing is like faint background noise and sometimes it stares us in the face, but it is always there, reminding us that we seek something more.

God understands our condition. In Isaiah 55:2–3 He admonishes,

> Why do you spend money for what is not bread, and your wages for what does not satisfy? Listen carefully to Me, and eat what is good, and let your soul delight itself in abundance. Incline your ear, and come to Me. Hear, and your soul shall live.

He is letting us know that only *He* has what we are looking for.

We long for Father God's blessing. We were created for blessing, and without it we develop a deep, insatiable inner hunger. Unless we look to God, we will not be satisfied. A human father's role is to protect, provide and establish his children's sense of identity. In a similar manner, Abba God intended that His blessing would impart into each heart His image of our identity ("Who am I?") and our destiny ("Why am I here?").

A Father's Blessing

The way Abba God blesses His children can be experienced through the blessing of a parent. My whole life and ministry changed when I received a blessing from my dad, Dr. Byung Kook Ahn. He went home to be with the Lord in 2010, and his life showed that he was a great man of God, the first Korean Southern Baptist pastor in America when he immigrated to the United States in 1958. But my upbringing was rocky, to say the least.

God showed me that I had bitterness toward my dad. So, in 1996, when my parents came to Pasadena from their home in Fairfax, Virginia, to attend my brother's wedding, I thought it was a good time to talk to him personally and ask his forgiveness for the wrongful attitudes I had toward him. I was dropping him off at the Pasadena Hilton to join my mother after we had watched some football together, and after I parked the car, I began to share my heart.

"Dad, before I begin, I want to say I deeply love you and honor you." I took a deep breath and continued. "But, Dad, I am still hurting over the rejection I felt when you physically punished me as I was growing up. I feel that you crossed the line, and as a fellow pastor, I realized that you had physically abused me. God also showed me that I am still bitter about this, and I want to repent before you and ask for your forgiveness." I had never confronted him on this issue before.

Sadness immediately came into his eyes. I could almost see tears welling up. "After all these years, you are still hurt over what happened when you were a kid?" he asked incredulously.

"Yes," I continued. "Dad, you don't have to respond to what I am sharing with you. Just getting this off my chest and expressing what I have wanted to say for a long time is healing enough." My father and I talked for several more minutes. He went into the hotel and I drove home.

A few minutes after I arrived home, my mother called. Now *she* was crying on the phone. But my mom was crying for me. "Ché, your dad told me what happened. Will you forgive me for not protecting you better when Dad was hitting you?" She went on, "As a pastor's wife and as an Asian woman, I couldn't intervene even though I wanted to."

I was shocked by what she was saying to me. This was the first time my mom had asked me to forgive her for anything. "Mom, I understand. There is nothing to forgive," I said.

Then she told me that my father wanted to talk to me and handed him the phone. My first thought was that Dad was mad at me for exposing him, and fear came into my heart. What happened next is something I will never forget for the rest of my life.

As my father picked up the phone, he said with deep tenderness and compassion words I had never heard him say or expected him to say: "Son, you just asked for forgiveness, but I realized I have never asked you for forgiveness. I realize that what I did to you as you were growing up was wrong. Will you forgive me?" he humbly asked.

I was stunned. I could hardly believe what I was hearing. I regained my composure enough to assure him that of course I forgave him. Then he added, "Son, you know how proud I am of you. And I love you very much."

What I was hearing shocked me. It was the first time I ever heard the words *I love you* from my dad. I did not know whether to cry, laugh or shout. "Dad, I love you, too," was my only reply. We said good-bye, and as soon as I hung up the phone, I started to dance around the house, pumping my arm and shouting, "Yes!" I was healed by my father's words of blessing.

Abba God began His relationship with us by giving a Father's blessing after creating Adam and Eve: "Then God blessed them and said, 'Be fruitful and multiply. Fill the earth and govern it. Reign over the fish in the sea, the birds in the sky, and all the animals that scurry along the ground'" (Genesis 1:28 NLT). Notice that God established both their identity and their destiny with this blessing.

Throughout the rest of this book, I will be inviting you to step forward and receive Father God's blessings. He wants to bless you. He has always had blessing in mind for you. Blessing is *His* idea, and nothing less than His blessing will ever satisfy the constant drive within you for what you have never been able to identify.

C. S. Lewis described our situation well: "If I find in myself a desire which no experience in this world can satisfy, the most probable explanation is that I was made for another world."[2]

You were made for another world—you were made for God's Kingdom and His blessings.

2

What Does Blessing Look Like?

We frequently use words without really understanding them; the words *bless* and *blessing* are two. Sneezing triggers an automatic "Bless you." When we get the last standby seat on a flight or find a great parking space, we feel "blessed." Running into an old acquaintance at a reunion can be an unexpected blessing—or, depending on your relationship, a "mixed blessing"! We frequently hear a blessing pronounced on special occasions. In prayer we ask God to bless others and us, our businesses, our countries, our food, etc. If we can name it, we want it blessed.

As we have seen, God created us to be blessed. Without His blessing, we experience restlessness within as we search for something more. But what is a blessing? What do *bless* and *blessing* really mean?

One Hebrew word for blessing is *esher*, which means "happiness." The Greek word for blessing, *makarios*, carries the same meaning. In both the Old and New Testaments, these words describe those who find their purpose and fulfillment in God. Scripture makes it clear that God's original design in creation was for humankind to experience prosperity, security and fulfillment (Genesis 1:28). In other words, He created us to be extremely happy.

Blessing in Ancient Cultures

As seen in many ancient cultures, the Israelites routinely blessed each other, both in greeting and in bidding good-bye. They frequently spoke blessings over others and all of their activities. Fathers blessed their children and wives. There were blessings for the safe birth of children, fertility of crops, increase of herds, defeat of enemies and long life. Leaders blessed their subjects and priests blessed worshipers. The Israelites believed that these spoken blessings carried actual power to confer positive good into their lives and the lives of others. Indeed, blessing is a form of prophesying God's intention for another. It originated with God, but humans were given His authority to bless in His name.

The use of blessing in the ongoing activities of daily life is well illustrated in the Old Testament book of Ruth, in which the widow Naomi, who has been living in a foreign country, decides to return to Israel after the death of her husband and two sons. She prays a blessing on her two foreign daughters-in-law, asking God to grant them the security of a new marriage (Ruth 1:8–9). One daughter-in-law, however, decides to return to Israel with Naomi.

In Israel, this daughter-in-law, Ruth, meets Boaz, one of Naomi's relatives. Boaz invokes a blessing for Ruth's well-being because of her faithfulness to Naomi (Ruth 2:11–12). When Ruth brings home a supply of grain she gleaned from Boaz's fields (a practice commanded by God to ensure the poor would not go hungry), Naomi prays God's blessing on Boaz. Boaz and Ruth eventually marry, and the villagers who witness the occasion ask God to bless the couple with children and prosper their household (Ruth 4:11–12). At the birth of their child, the women bless God for dealing bountifully with Naomi (Ruth 4:14–15). Ruth, the great-grandmother to King David, has a privileged position in the lineage of Christ.

These are just a few of the many blessings in the book of Ruth. They show that the ancient Israelites were constantly aware of God's presence in their everyday activities and that they wanted His active involvement in their lives. Because of our casual use of *bless* and *blessing*, we have lost the significance of inviting the actual presence of God and the prophetic power of blessing, destiny and favor into our daily lives and activities.

What Is a Blessing?

The implied power in a blessing explains why the Israelites frequently blessed themselves and others. They knew that they were speaking divine favor over a person or circumstance, with the intention of promoting welfare and happiness. To be blessed is to be favored by God—God wants you to walk in His favor! In effect, an ancient blessing was a decree that God's intentions would come forth in all fullness for the person being blessed. A person who blessed stood in agreement with God's intentions to confer good upon a person or circumstance.

Blessings are central to God's nature. They have roots in His love and His desire for our happiness—not in our merit or performance. In this sense they are unconditional and available to every person. But blessings do not automatically fall on us; to obtain blessings we must understand their existence and power and actively choose to receive them when they are released.

Blessings are not just a verbal exchange of positive thoughts between two people. They are not simply compliments or words of encouragement, nor are they a form of positive thinking or a way to wish another person good luck. Real blessings contain spiritual substance and have prophetic power to produce positive change. When you understand what blessings are designed to produce and how they operate, you will be able to effectively receive them into your own life and declare them into the lives of others.

The Power of Blessing

You have the power to bless yourself and others. Through blessing, you have the power to radically alter a person's life and circumstances, as we see in the life of a boy named Ben.

As a young black child living in inner-city Detroit, Ben looked like an early failure waiting to happen. His parents divorced when he was eight, and he reacted to the loss of his father by becoming angry and aggressive. He had a violent temper and frequently assaulted his peers at the slightest provocation.

Ben struggled academically, becoming increasingly discouraged with each passing year. By fourth grade, he was at the bottom of his class and totally disinterested in learning. Ben's mother, a single parent with little education and no real employment skills, worked two and three jobs to make ends meet. Often this meant she was away from home from 5 a.m. to 11 p.m., and he would go days at a time without seeing her.

Ben seemed to be on the fast track to dropping out of school and getting involved with substance abuse and/or gang membership. But he had a powerful advantage that many children in his position lack: Ben's mother believed that her son was blessed by God to do something important. She believed in Ben and had positive expectations for him. She limited his television time, made his outdoor play contingent on completing homework and required him to read two library books each week and write a written book report.

Ben would certainly have rebelled at this regimen, but his mother did one more all-important thing. She constantly encouraged him and praised his efforts. She was convinced that he would go far, and she kept reminding him that he could become anything he chose to work for. She displayed interest in the books he read and scrutinized his written reports carefully, even though she herself could not read—she pretended to read just to hold him accountable! Ben's mother frequently told him he was blessed by God and would accomplish something important in life. She may not have realized this, but she was prophesying destiny and greatness into his life.

Spurred on by his mother's approval and blessing, Ben began to love reading and the world of knowledge it opened to him. By the end of fifth grade, he was at the top of his class, amazing his teachers. He graduated with top honors from high school, attended Yale and went on to medical school. This man—Dr. Ben Carson—became the director of pediatric neurosurgery at Johns Hopkins at the young age of 33. In 1987 he gained international acclaim by becoming the first neurosurgeon to successfully separate eight-month-old twins joined at the head.[1]

Ben Carson's story is more than a heartwarming tale; it is a striking example of the prophetic power of blessing in the life and destiny of a person. Ben's mother continually planted positive words about him in his mind and heart. The power of her blessing opened the doors of a great destiny for her son.

You may or may not have had someone like Ben Carson's mother encouraging and blessing you as a child. In fact, about now you may be thinking, *I wish I had someone like that at my back. Someone who really believed in me and encouraged me.* I have good news: Abba God believes in you completely and wants you to have a great destiny:

> You [Father God] have given him his heart's desire, and have not withheld the request of his lips. For you meet him with the blessings of goodness. . . . You have made him most blessed forever; You have made him exceedingly glad with Your presence.
>
> Psalm 21:2–3, 6

God wants to bless you! His heart overflows with love for you, and your happiness is important to Him. Read on and discover how you can experience the unconditional goodness of your Father God.

3

God Is Good

One of my favorite authors, A. W. Tozer, wrote, "What comes into our minds when we think about God is the most important thing about us."[1]

A few years ago, in a survey conducted by Baylor University, 1,700 people filled out a checklist of characteristics they felt were most descriptive of God. Overall, 92 percent of the respondents believed in some type of God or higher power; within this majority, four distinct aspects of God's personality and engagement in human affairs dominated the respondents' thinking.

The most popular view (31 percent) saw God as an authoritarian deity involved in the details of every creature's life and the world affairs of humans. Those with this perspective believe God is continually angered by human acts of sin and ready to release judgment on ungodly persons.

The next most common description (24 percent) defined God as a distant cosmic force that launched creation but then left it alone. Close behind at 23 percent were those respondents who saw God as a benevolent deity who sets absolute standards for humanity but is also forgiving. While He is ultimately in control, He offers multiple chances for humans to correct their ways.

The smallest group of respondents (16 percent) saw God as critical, keeping a judgmental eye on the world. At the same time, they do not see Him as actively involved in human affairs and do not believe He intervenes to punish or comfort people.[2]

I was disappointed with the survey results, because most saw God as judgmental, critical, detached and harsh. What they did not see is part of the essence of God's nature and character: His goodness.

How could that many survey respondents so blatantly miss the characteristic of God being good? Unfortunately, the Church has presented God negatively so often that many believe God is angry with them and seeks to punish them. Even many regular church attenders see God in a legalistic way—a demanding deity who does all kinds of things that do not make sense, but who is still supposed to be worshiped as a loving being. I am amazed how many Christians do not believe that God is on their side!

Perhaps you identify with one of the four respondent groups in the Baylor survey. Maybe the idea that God is good, that He loves you and wants to bless you—that He is not angry with you—is new information. You may be thinking, *Surely God reserves His blessings for people who do good things and deserve to be blessed.* Would you be surprised to learn that God offers His blessings freely to all without any regard to merit? No person is ever blessed based on his or her performance. Blessings are available to us because of who God is.

How Good Is God?

In order to understand the relationship between God and blessings, we need to begin with God's goodness. Maybe you have heard this popular Christian saying:

> God is good all the time.
> All the time God is good.

What do we mean when we say God is good? And how good is God's goodness? Apparently, to God His goodness is so central to His character that when the prophet Moses asked God to reveal His most intimate self, God responded, "I will make all My goodness pass before you" (Exodus 33:18–19).

In showing His goodness to Moses, God was sharing the most important aspect of Himself. He wanted Moses to understand who He was and what He was truly like. God's goodness is so good—so unique to Him—that it finds expression in a special Hebrew word, *hesed*. *Hesed* is mentioned in connection with God 240 times in the Old Testament. There are no words in English that truly contain its full meaning; we must combine three basic characteristics—strength, steadfastness and love—in order to capture the Hebrew concept of *hesed*.[3] Strength conveys that God's goodness is truthful, loyal and faithful. Steadfastness refers to God's unchanging devotion and His love seen in concrete acts of kindness and favor as He fulfills His promises. In Scripture *hesed* is frequently translated "lovingkindness" or "tender mercies."

The word *hesed* also implies personal involvement and commitment in a lifelong covenant relationship—not unlike marriage. Marriage is a covenant relationship with oaths that are binding on both parties, but real marital love completely transcends its legalistic boundaries. God frequently describes His goodness (*hesed*) toward His people in terms of a marriage relationship. No matter how much we falter in our commitment to Him, He is always faithful in His goodness to us.

God asserts the faithfulness of His goodness (*hesed*) in Deuteronomy 7:9 (NLT):

Understand, therefore, that the LORD your God is indeed God. He is the faithful God who keeps his covenant for a thousand generations and lavishes his unfailing love [*hesed*] on those who love him and obey his commands.

It is His goodness, His *hesed*, that caused creation to come into existence (Psalm 136:5–9). His goodness sent Christ into the world to reconcile us back into a relationship with Him (John 3:16) and continues to offer us every good thing (Romans 8:31–32). Thus, we see it was His goodness that brought us—and the entire universe—into being. He is for us and wants to give us everything that will fulfill us and make us happy.

How can we possibly describe this degree of goodness? A few years ago, my wife, Sue, and I flew to Colorado Springs in February. We were in the Rockies when the temperature hit minus 40 degrees Fahrenheit. That is 40 degrees *below zero*—a record cold. On the tarmac, Sue began to cry and said, "I want to turn around and go home. Can you get me a ticket to fly home right now?" She was only half joking. I told her I would check with the service desk at United Airlines. She decided to stay, but without exaggeration it was the coldest weather we have experienced anytime, anywhere. Did I mention that it was cold?

But it was far from absolute cold, minus 459.7 degrees Fahrenheit. Even though we could not feel it, some warmth was still in the air at minus 40 degrees. But absolute cold means no warmth is left at all; cold is all there is. I think it is the same with God's goodness. His *hesed* is absolute goodness—strong, steadfast and totally loving, without any fluctuations. His goodness is all there is.

How good is God? Absolutely good, absolutely all the time.

Blessing Is God's Idea

Most of you have heard of Facebook. When you create a Facebook page, you become a member of a worldwide community. Besides posting basic information about yourself, you can share your interests, involvement in sports, personal philosophy, recreational activities and photos. It is a way of letting others know you and what is happening in your life.

You might say that blessings are the equivalent of a Facebook page for God; they are a way He makes Himself known to us. Through blessings, God shows us His goodness—the essence of Himself. He makes His intention and purpose for us clear when He blesses. And with each blessing, He encourages us to experience more of His goodness: "Oh, taste and see that the LORD is good; blessed is the man who trusts in Him!" (Psalm 34:8). As we grow in our knowledge and understanding of God's nature and character, we become increasingly able to see, believe and receive more of His blessings.

It is striking how frequently the word "blessing" appears throughout the Bible; it may be the most frequently mentioned activity associated with God in Scripture. The theme of blessing is found more than 400 times in the Old Testament and 65 times in the New Testament. Everywhere blessing is synonymous with God; when He shows up, so does blessing. Blessing is so intrinsic to God that we could say it is God's nature to bless.

Through receiving His blessings, we become more aware of His presence with us, and our confidence and joy in Him grow. Participating in His blessings confirms to us that God is thinking about us favorably. He wants us to know that we are on His mind all the time: "How precious also are Your thoughts to me, O God! How vast is the sum of them! If I should count them, they would outnumber the sand" (Psalm 139:17–18 NASB). He makes it clear that we have *always* been on His mind: "Before I formed you in the womb I knew you, before you were born I set you apart" (Jeremiah 1:5 NIV). His thoughts are full of wonderful plans for us (Jeremiah 29:11).

God's goodness is so complete and bountiful that blessings flow from His nature to us in a constant and undiluted stream. Blessings are not so much something that God *does* as they are the outflowing of something that He *is*. Abba God is inviting us into a relationship to share that outflowing with Him. The blessings we receive are not simply discrete gifts from Him or tools for making our lives and the lives of those around us better. They actually serve as an invitation to commune with God Himself and enter our rightful place as heirs of His Kingdom, seated in heavenly places with Him.

I hope you will see your relationship with Father God in a new way. I want you to understand the purpose of God's blessings for you, and I pray that you will be set on fire with the joyful expectation of a blessed life!

4

God's Blessings on Israel

God has an agenda in blessing you. His purpose is seen from the beginning, when Abba God blessed Adam and Eve so they would fill the earth with their offspring: "Then God blessed them, and God said to them, 'Be fruitful and multiply; fill the earth and subdue it; have dominion over . . . every living thing that moves on the earth'" (Genesis 1:28).

God's intention was for the generations that followed Adam and Eve to experience paradise. The Garden in Eden was paradise; it was heaven on earth. There was no sickness, disease, pain, suffering or poverty; instead there was abundance, goodness, peace, joy and intimate fellowship with God. As Adam and Eve multiplied and filled the earth, the Garden would have expanded with the growth of the population and eventually covered the whole earth. Heaven would kiss earth forever. The whole earth would have been "filled with the knowledge of the glory of the LORD" (Habakkuk 2:14).

Paradise was lost when man sinned, but God's purpose remains the same. Remember, it is His nature to manifest His love and goodness by blessing His children.

To begin the process of restoring what was lost (see Acts 3:19–21), Abba God chose another family, headed by Abraham and Sarah, to receive His blessing so that all the families of the earth would be blessed through them. In His covenant with Abraham He promised, "I will make you into a great nation. I will bless you and make you famous, and you will be a blessing to others. . . . All the families on earth will be blessed through you" (Genesis 12:2–3 NLT). God meant for His people—the Jewish people and later the Church—to be a blessing to all the peoples of the earth.

The Jewish Phenomenon

If you have a hard time accepting that God blesses the Jewish people, consider this: At least 20 percent of Nobel Prize winners have been Jews, even though Jews constitute less than 0.2 percent of the world's population.[1]

The book *The Jewish Phenomenon* affirms this outsized Jewish presence among Nobel Prize recipients and shows other evidence of God's blessing on the Jewish people.

Among the Jews who have been blessed with wealth and influence are the following:

- 45 percent of the top forty Forbes richest Americans
- 33 percent of American multimillionaires
- 20 percent of professors at leading universities
- 40 percent of partners in the leading law firms in New York and Washington[2]

Much of God's blessing is connected with multiplication and abundance (see Deuteronomy 28:4, for example). In Deuteronomy 7:13–14, we read this promise:

> He will love you and bless you and multiply you; He will also bless the fruit of your womb and the fruit of your land, your grain and your new wine and your oil, the increase of your cattle and the offspring of your flock, in the land of which He swore to your fathers to give you. You shall be blessed above all peoples; there shall not be a male or female barren among you or among your livestock.

If part of God's blessing is financial prosperity, there is no question that the Jews are blessed. I noticed this even as I was growing up. The Jews lived in nicer homes and drove nicer cars, like the Cadillac owned by my best friend Billy's parents (my parents drove a used Chevy). My closest friends, who were Jews, all lived on the other, nicer side of Rock Creek

Park. I cannot recall one Jewish friend that lived on my side of Rock Creek Park.

Some reading this, especially secular Jews, may disagree. I have talked with many during my visits to Israel who have become agnostics. If there is no God, then there is no blessing from God. They point to historical persecution of the Jewish people, culminating in the Holocaust, as proof. If God existed, why would He allow the Holocaust?

My take on this is not that God has cursed the Jews. God's covenant with them has not changed over the centuries. Satan, however, comes to kill, steal and destroy (see John 10:10), and he knows the way to hurt God is by attacking His children. Jews and Christians throughout history have been severely persecuted and still are. Yet any reasonable person who sees Christians in the Middle East hunted by the terrorist movement that calls itself the Islamic State would not come to the conclusion that Christians are cursed because of the persecution. In fact, Jesus taught, "Blessed are those who are persecuted for righteousness' sake, for theirs is the kingdom of heaven" (Matthew 5:10). Persecuted Christian martyrs are blessed in this life and the life to come. Our ultimate blessing comes when we are with Jesus for eternity—as Paul says, "To die is gain" (Philippians 1:21). The Word of God is true; however, the devil may try to thwart it. God has blessed the family line of Abraham— the Jewish people—and that blessing remains on God's people.

Some of the clearest evidence of God's blessing on the Jews is the restoration of the land of Palestine to the Jews and the reestablishment of Israel as a nation on May 14, 1948, after two thousand years. Our apostolic network, Harvest International Ministry, leads an annual tour of Israel. I have visited eight times, and every time I am amazed at how prosperous this nation has become in a relatively short amount of time. While Israel is not yet free from national security issues and tensions in the Gaza Strip and West Bank, the bottom line is that you can see God's hand of blessing on it. It won both the 1967 Six-Day War and the 1973 Yom Kippur War against great odds, and today it has become one of the most prosperous and powerful nations in the entire Middle East. Israel has achieved this prosperity without the natural petroleum resources that some of the other Middle Eastern nations have enjoyed. God has truly blessed the Jewish people.

A final example comes from one of my favorite columnists, Joel Stein—himself Jewish—who published an amusing yet true piece in the *Los Angeles Times* about how Jews run Hollywood:

> Only 22% of Americans now believe "the movie and television industries are pretty much run by Jews," down from nearly 50% in 1964. The Anti-Defamation League . . . sees in these numbers a victory against stereotyping. Actually, it just shows how dumb America has gotten. Jews totally run Hollywood.[3]

Stein goes on to list a remarkably high number of Hollywood executives—whose companies include Paramount Pictures, Walt Disney Co., Warner Bros., and MGM—that are Jewish.

Here is some good news: If you are a born-again believer, you are a descendant of Abraham who has been "grafted in" to the blessing of God through Jesus Christ (see Romans 11:16–18). In Galatians 3:13–14, the apostle Paul writes,

> Christ has redeemed us from the curse of the law, having become a curse for us (for it is written, "Cursed is everyone who hangs on a tree"), that the blessing of Abraham might come upon the Gentiles in Christ Jesus, that we might receive the promise of the Spirit through faith.

The blessing of Abraham is now with all who believe in Jesus as their Lord, Messiah and Savior. God loves you and demonstrated that love by sending Jesus, our substitute. He became a curse for us so that we might encounter the fullness of His blessing. In the next chapter, I want to share this good news in detail so that you can further appreciate what God has done for you and for the world.

5

The Great Exchange of the Cross

When I was growing up, the game show *Let's Make a Deal* was quite popular. Contestants would exchange something they brought for a mystery prize behind one of three doors. The name of the game has changed over the years, but the concept is still popular today. The show *Deal or No Deal* comes to mind, in which contestants choose a case containing an unknown amount of money. They can keep the case or exchange it for offers from an unseen banker. The key that keeps viewers watching is the suspense of not knowing what lies behind the door or inside the cases.

The Foundation for All Blessings

There is no mystery when it comes to the exchange that God wants to make with you. If your life is full of discouragement, sickness, oppression, poverty, addictions, anxiety, fear and stress, He wants to exchange it for a life of abundance (John 10:10), prosperity (3 John 2), healing (Acts 10:38) and joy and peace (Romans 14:17).

The foundation for all of life's blessings given in exchange for your problems is Jesus' dying on the cross for you. Let's briefly list some of the exchanges that took place on the cross.

Jesus was punished so that you could be forgiven; He became sin so that you could be made righteous.

One of the most powerful verses in the Bible shows the exchange of our sin so that we might become right with God: "For He made Him who knew no sin to be sin for us, that we might become the righteousness of God in Him" (2 Corinthians 5:21).

Sin is the root cause of all of your problems and the world's problems. Everything was perfect until Adam and Eve sinned in the Garden. Since then, sin has been the most devastating curse on humanity. In the words of the renowned Billy Graham:

> The most devastating fact in the universe is sin. The cause of all troubles, the root of all sorrow, the dread of every man lies in this one small word—sin. All mental disorders, all sicknesses, all destruction, all wars find their root in sin. Sin is madness in the brain, poison in the heart. . . . It is a raging torrent that sweeps everything before it.[1]

The good news is that Jesus became sin for us that we might be forgiven and delivered from its curse:

> But sin overreached itself on the cross. Man's hideous injustice that crucified Christ became the means that opened the way for man to become free. Sin's masterpiece of shame and hate became God's masterpiece of mercy and forgiveness. Through the death of Christ upon the cross, sin itself was crucified for those who believe in Him. Sin was conquered on the cross. His death is the foundation of our hope, the promise of our triumph! . . . He proved the truth of all God's promises to man; and if you will accept Christ by faith today you, too, can be forgiven for your sins.[2]

Jesus was separated from and rejected by the Father so that you could be adopted as His son or daughter.

Jesus made four significant statements on the cross. The first—"Father, forgive them, for they know not what they do"—encompassed all of mankind. Jesus drew a circle that included everyone who has ever lived. His second word from the cross was directed toward a thief hanging next to him: "This day you will be with me in paradise." This declaration drew a smaller circle to include all who have repented, come to Christ and been forgiven by God. Though still a wide circle, it is smaller than the first.

The third word from the cross—"Woman, behold thy son. Son, behold thy mother"—drew an even smaller circle. It refers to those who are not only saved but have taken upon themselves the responsibilities of authentic and disciplined discipleship.

With the fourth word from the cross, there are no more circles. From this point on, Jesus spoke only of Himself and of His relationship to His Father. At the ninth hour, after hours of silence, Jesus exclaimed, "My God, My God, why have You forsaken Me?" (Matthew 27:46). At that point, Jesus, who knew only perfect intimacy with Abba God, was separated from and rejected by God the Father for the first time in all of eternity—so that we could be accepted as sons and daughters.

Our adoption into His family is confirmed in two key passages: The first is 1 John 3:1 (NIV): "See what great love the Father has lavished on us, that we should be called children of God!" And children we are. The second passage is Romans 8:15–17 (NASB):

> For you have not received a spirit of slavery leading to fear again, but you have received a spirit of adoption as sons by which we cry out, "Abba! Father!" The Spirit Himself testifies with our spirit that we are children of God, and if children, heirs also, heirs of God and fellow heirs with Christ, if indeed we suffer with Him so that we may also be glorified with Him.

By the Holy Spirit, we can come to Abba God with confidence and know with assurance that we are His children.

Jesus took our sickness and pain so that we could be healed.

Isaiah prophesied that the Messiah would take up our sickness and our pains on the cross:

> Surely he took up our pain[3] and bore our suffering,[4] yet we considered him punished by God, stricken by him, and afflicted. But he was pierced for our transgressions, he was crushed for our iniquities; the punishment that brought us peace was on him, and by his wounds we are healed.
>
> Isaiah 53:4–5 NIV

The word *wounds* (or, in some translations, *stripes*) in verse 5 literally means "bruise." It signifies the entire wounding or bruising of Jesus, including the stripes laid on His back, the crown of thorns on His head, the nails that pierced His hands and feet and the spear that pierced His side. He endured all this bodily suffering for our physical healing.

The apostle Peter affirms this in 1 Peter 2:24: "By whose stripes you were healed" (the Greek word *iaomai* refers to physical healing). We also see it in Matthew 8:16–17 (NIV):

> When evening came, many who were demon-possessed were brought to him, and he drove out the spirits with a word and healed all the sick. This was to fulfill what was spoken through the prophet Isaiah: "He took up our infirmities and bore our diseases."

The exchange of healing that took place on the cross was prophetically and metaphorically demonstrated among the people of Israel, who rebelled in the wilderness and came under the judgment of being bitten by poisonous snakes. When the people repented, God instructed how they could be healed: He told Moses to "make a snake and put it up on a pole; anyone who is bitten can look at it and live" (Numbers 21:8 NIV). That pole represents the cross and the snake Jesus, who became our sickness and pain so that everyone who looks to the cross would be healed. Jesus testified to this in the gospel of John: "As Moses lifted up the serpent in the wilderness, even so must the Son of Man be lifted up, that whoever believes in Him should not perish but have eternal life" (John 3:14–15).

Decreeing God's healing through the cross releases power. I was healed of a jaw muscle disorder known as TMJ through declaring over my jaw that "by His stripes, I am healed." The issue began when Sue and I went to see a Billy Graham outreach movie on the life of Joni Eareckson Tada. Right in the middle of the movie, my jaw locked up and I felt excruciating pain—I wanted to scream. I ran to the men's room to see if I could manipulate my jaw back into the socket, even though I knew nothing had happened to knock it out of place. I did not know what was happening.

We left the theater and I called my future brother-in-law, Dr. John Casler, a brilliant and skillful surgeon. He examined me and said I had TMJ. I had never heard of it before.

He told me it was arthritis of the jaw. "I'm too young to have arthritis!" was my response. I was only 24. He told me I would have to take Advil for the rest of my life and that surgery was out of the question.

Yet something rose up within me. "This is not of God," I declared. "I refuse TMJ!" I made a covenant with God; every time I saw myself in the mirror, I was going to declare, "By His stripes, I am healed." I would do this three or four times a day.

This lasted for a year and a half. Sometimes we quit too soon and give up early when we need to "fight the good fight of faith" (1 Timothy 6:12). One morning, as I woke up and yawned to welcome the new day, my jaw was instantly healed. I had full movement and flexibility, and I was pain free for the first time since that day in the theater.

Jesus became a curse for us so that we might be delivered from all curses.

Galatians 3:13–14 (NASB) is a key verse for this whole book:

Christ redeemed us from the curse of the Law, having become a curse for us—for it is written, "Cursed is everyone who hangs on a tree"—in order that in Christ Jesus the blessing of Abraham might come to the Gentiles, so that we would receive the promise of the Spirit through faith.

The curse of the law results from breaking the law, violating God's Word, which man has done since the Garden of Eden. Jesus became a curse for us so that the blessing of Abraham can come to those who believe in Jesus as Lord.

Jesus bore the curse for us, but we have to appropriate our deliverance from curses through personal deliverances and decrees. God delivered me from the curse of drug addiction when I gave my life to Jesus, but other issues in my life later surfaced. One of these, which I call a generational curse, emerged when I was married and a new father. Though my dad was a wonderful and godly man, he had a major anger problem. It would often manifest when he had to discipline me; instead of spanking, he would physically abuse me. One time he hit me with a broomstick until the stick broke in half.

Sins and resulting curses can be passed down from one generation to another. One day, when my son was around four, he did something to upset me—to be honest with you, I cannot remember what he did, but what I did to him I will never forget. As soon as he had disobeyed, I picked him up by one leg. I was ready to beat him with my hands when the Lord stopped me. *Look what you are doing to your son. You are doing the same thing that your father did to you. You need to break this curse of anger and violence.* I was stunned. I put Gabriel down and fell on my knees, weeping and repenting. I renounced the spirit of anger and abuse, and something supernatural happened. I felt as if a demonic spirit left me. I was never the same. I got up from my knees a changed man.

From that day forward, I cannot remember a time when I physically abused any of my four children. God broke that curse over my life. He can do that over your life as well, whether you are under a curse of sickness, immorality, divorce, poverty, drug addiction or alcoholism.

Many Christians have prodigal sons and daughters because they are ignorant of their authority to break the curse of generational sins. I have determined and decreed that the sins of my bloodlines end with me. None of my generational sins have to be passed down to my children or to my children's children.

Jesus became poor for us so that we might be rich.

In my book *The Grace of Giving*, I make this statement:

> Numerous passages in the New Testament make it clear that the same blessing that God bestowed upon Abraham was made available to Gentile believers through Jesus Christ. We are told that Christ became poor for our sake, so that we might become rich, and that all the blessings of Abraham, which includes prosperity, are ours in Christ Jesus.[5]

This idea is summed up in 2 Corinthians 8:9: "For you know the grace of our Lord Jesus Christ, that though He was rich, yet for your sakes He became poor, that you through His poverty might become rich."

Commentators have a hard time with this passage because they read it with a religious spirit of poverty. They spiritualize the verse, interpreting Jesus' poverty as spiritual poverty (that is, He became man) and our riches as spiritual riches. I believe most scholars interpret it this way because of a curse of poverty prevalent in the Body of Christ, leading to a "poverty mentality" and a distorted perspective on life. In context, 2 Corinthians 8:9 appears within two whole chapters dealing with money; the plain meaning of the verse in context is that Paul was talking about *actual money*. But some have a hard time seeing that God wants us to be financially rich—for example, a note in the margin of 2 Corinthians 8:9 in the Thompson Chain-Reference Bible gives the interpretation "spiritual riches." Matthew Henry also explains away the meaning: "Rich in the love of God, rich in the blessings of the new covenant, rich in the hopes of eternal life."[6]

I refute this interpretation of Scripture. Contrary to popular belief, Jesus was not poor. Though He was an itinerant rabbi, He had a large following, and His ministry received support from wealthy people (several of whom are explicitly mentioned in Luke 8:1–3). Jesus was frequently entertained by influential members of society and also had close friends, like Lazarus, who were rich. While Jesus cautioned against the idolatry of wealth, He never advocated poverty as a way of life. In fact, He gave hope to the poor by promising that theirs was the Kingdom of heaven (see Luke 6:20).

I used to think just like the commentators until God broke the curse of poverty over my life beginning in 1996. It began with an encounter I share in my book *The Grace of Giving*, when a friend I had known for years invited me to speak at the church he pastored, which was interested in becoming a part of HIM.

> After I spoke, my friend pulled me aside and confronted me with this truth, in love. He said to me, "Ché, since I have been with you over the weekend, I have picked up that you have a spirit of poverty. . . . I believe that God wants to break the spirit of poverty and start to prosper you. I want to do a prophetic act. I know that you only spoke one time, but I want to give you an honorarium for five thousand dollars. This is prophetic to let you know that God does not want you to limit Him in any way in how much you make. Second, by giving you this, I break the spirit of poverty over your life!"[7]

Five thousand dollars was the largest sum I had ever received for one message. When my friend made a decree over my life, something shifted. Later, Cindy Jacobs prayed for me, and I received deliverance from the curse of poverty.[8]

Jesus became poor at the cross so that we might have the abundance He promised in John 10:10, which includes financial prosperity.

Finally, Jesus died our death so that we could have eternal life.

The most famous Scripture in the Bible, which Martin Luther called "the gospel in miniature," is John 3:16–17 (NIV):

For God so loved the world that he gave his one and only Son, that whoever believes in him shall not perish but have eternal life. For God did not send his Son into the world to condemn the world, but to save the world through him.

The Bible also says in Romans 5:8 (NIV), "But God demonstrates his own love for us in this: While we were still sinners, Christ died for us."

A number of years ago, I heard about a U.S. veteran of the wars in Iraq and Afghanistan who listened to a preacher expounding on how Christ laid down His life for us, who were enemies of God, so that we could have eternal life. The soldier said to the pastor, "I am not impressed with your Jesus. I just came back from Iraq, and as we were sweeping a building, looking for the enemy, my buddy and I came into a room with a suicide bomber. As soon as my friend saw the bomb strapped to his body, he jumped onto the man to protect me and my friends, and he was blown to pieces during that act. My friend was no saint. What makes your Jesus better than my friend?"

The pastor answered with wisdom. "What your friend did for you was extremely heroic. But the Bible says we were the enemies of God when He died for us. Your friend gave his life for you and his other friends, but he would not have died for the Iraqi terrorist. That is the difference between Jesus and your friend."

If you have never experienced the life Jesus exchanged for yours on the cross, why not start by doing what Jesus taught in Matthew 10:39? "He who finds his life will lose it, and he who loses his life for My sake will find it." Essentially Jesus makes this offer: "I will give you My life if you give Me your life," which is something like saying, "I will give you my Rolls-Royce for your beat-up Volkswagen that has flat tires." Is this not good news? His offer was only made possible because Jesus went to the cross, where the ultimate exchange took place. That is why He went to the cross with love and joy.

If you want to exchange your life for His blessed, abundant and eternal life, pause right now and pray this prayer with all your heart:

Jesus, forgive me for my sins. I give You my heart, my whole life. I make You the Lord of my life. By Your grace, I will follow You and obey You all the days of my life. In Jesus' name, amen.

6

The Purpose of God's Blessing

God wants to bless you so that you can be a blessing to those who do not know Jesus. One of the most powerful Psalms—perhaps one of the most powerful chapters in the entire Bible—is Psalm 67:

> God be merciful to us and bless us, and cause His face to shine upon us, that Your way may be known on earth, Your salvation among all nations. Let the peoples praise You, O God; let all the peoples praise You. Oh, let the nations be glad and sing for joy! For You shall judge the people righteously, and govern the nations on earth. Let the peoples praise You, O God; let all the peoples praise You. Then the earth shall yield her increase; God, our own God, shall bless us. God shall bless us, and all the ends of the earth shall fear Him.

"Blessed to Be a Blessing"

Let me give you a running commentary on this psalm. The psalmist begins by petitioning God to bless the nation of Israel, a petition that echoes the Aaronic blessing of Numbers 6:24–26:

> The LORD bless you and keep you; the LORD make His face shine upon you, and be gracious to you; the LORD lift up His countenance upon you, and give you peace.

One difference between Psalm 67 and Aaron's blessing is that the focus of the psalm in not on "you" but "us." God wants you to ask for blessing on yourself *and* your family. (We will do this in part 2 when we speak decrees over our lives and our loved ones.)

In Psalm 67 the writer asks for God's face to shine upon His people. In the Old Testament, the face of God is a metaphor for His favor (see Psalms 4:6–7; 31:16; 44:3; 80:3, 7, 19) and also His presence. When the presence and favor of God come, God's blessings are manifested. We find a good example of this in 2 Samuel 6: David tried to bring the Ark of the Covenant—which represents God's presence—to Jerusalem. But because David did not read the "owner's manual" and mishandled the Ark, judgment came. Out of fear and in an attempt to figure out what to do next, David stored the Ark at the home of Obed-Edom. The result? "The LORD blessed Obed-Edom and all his household" (2 Samuel 6:11). With His presence comes the blessing of God.

The striking part of Psalm 67 is how the writer affirms that the purpose of the blessing is to bring salvation to the nations: "God be merciful to us *and bless us*, and cause His face to shine upon us, that Your way may be known on earth, *Your salvation among all nations*" (verses 1–2, emphasis mine). This affirmation of God's blessing serves as a reminder of His covenant that He made with Abraham. The point is that God wants to bless you in such an extreme way that it will bring salvation to the nations.

One way in which salvation will come to unbelievers is through blessing those who do not know Jesus. Early on in my ministry, God showed me the power of blessing those who did not know Him. It was a hot, humid summer morning in the nation's capital. A heat wave over the country had recently claimed the lives of many of the elderly. The temperature was approaching 100 degrees at nine in the morning as I heard the trash collectors drive up our road. I heard the Holy Spirit whisper into my heart to give the trash collectors something cold to drink. I ran out of my room to look for my wife.

"Honey, do we have anything cold to drink?" I asked.

"No, but we have some frozen orange juice," Sue answered. "I can make it quick."

"The trash collectors are hot, and I felt the Lord say, 'Give them something to drink.'"

Sue grabbed a good stack of paper cups and gave me the pitcher of orange juice. I ran out of the house, placed the cups and juice on the hood of my car and ran after the collectors, who had already passed our house.

They saw me waving them down. "Guys, it's a hot day," I greeted them. "I have some cold orange juice down at my house. Why don't you take a little break and come on over?"

They looked at each other skeptically. After all, who cares about trash collectors? After recovering from the shock of the invitation, they proceeded to follow me to the house. I poured a cup for the four perspiring but grateful men. As they drank, I began to share with them. "You know, years ago I would never have stopped to help anyone but myself. I was a drug addict. But then I surrendered my life to Jesus, and He has completely changed my life. I just want to let you know that Jesus loves you very much."

The men smiled, thanked me for the drink and went back to work. No fireworks. No one got on his knees to repent. The Gospel was simply demonstrated through a kind act of blessing and a short testimony. I forgot about the incident until three months later.

My wife and I had bought our first home that September. As we were unpacking our boxes, trash began to overflow. I knew that the trash collectors had their work cut out for them as they approached our house, and I thought, *Why not bless them with a little continental breakfast on our new patio?* Sue and I took out some juice, I bought a dozen doughnuts and we set them nicely on our patio table and waited for the trash collectors to arrive.

I met them in front of our house and said, "We just moved in, and with all the trash here, we thought we could return the favor by inviting you men to a little continental breakfast on our patio."

You should have seen the look on their faces—an "Is this guy for real?" look. They assured me the policy was to take all the trash of a newly moved-in neighbor. But everything was set up, so I invited them anyway, and they happily followed me to our patio table. As they munched on their doughnuts, I began to share my faith.

"I would have never done this several years ago," I started, "but since then I have given my life to Jesus Christ, and I—"

Before I could finish my sentence, one of the trash collectors interrupted. "Didn't you use to live on Georgia Avenue?"

"Why, yes," I said.

"You're the guy who gave me and my friends some orange juice on that hot summer day."

"Why, yes, I am."

"Well, I want to shake your hand," he said, reaching out his hand toward mine. "I want to thank you for blessing us with that orange juice that day. You made such an impression on me that a few weeks later I went to a Christian meeting with a friend who invited me. I gave my life to Jesus there. I wanted to come by your house and thank you, but I was transferred to this new neighborhood. I can't believe that you moved into my new route! Thank you for planting that seed in my life."

I was stunned. I started to praise God for His goodness and faithfulness. At the same time, I smiled at God's sense of humor. Who could have orchestrated that—a man comes to know the Lord after I blessed him with a little bit of kindness, he gets transferred to a new neighborhood and *then* I run into him after buying my first home? Only God.

Blessing for the Purpose of Reformation

Psalm 67 presents more than a prayer for blessing and salvation. This is a reformer's prayer. The psalmist wants the blessing of God to teach the nations the ways of God: "That Your *way* may be known on earth" (verse 2, emphasis mine). In Psalm 103:7, we see that the Lord "made known His *ways* to Moses, His acts to the children of Israel" (emphasis mine). Moses had the wisdom to know God's heart, not just His acts and miracles, in the wilderness.

God wants His people to show the world how to do life according to His ways. How do you have a great marriage according to God's ways? How do you parent and raise up a godly generation? How do you do business with integrity? How do you govern a nation or city without corruption and compromise? You can show the ways of God only if you are walking in His ways and living out this blessing. The world is asking these questions, and the Bible prophesies that one day the nations will seek His ways through God's house, His people:

> Now it shall come to pass in the latter days that the mountain of the LORD's house shall be established on the top of the mountains, and shall be exalted above the hills; and all nations shall flow to it. Many people shall come and say, "Come, and let us go up to the mountain of the LORD, to the house of the God of Jacob; He will teach us His ways, and we shall walk in His paths." For out of Zion shall go forth the law.
>
> Isaiah 2:2–3

The psalmist asks for God's blessing on His people so that they, in turn, can disciple the nations.

The middle of Psalm 67 is consumed by worship and praise. Praise and thanksgiving are the language of faith. In faith the psalmist declares that God has heard his prayers, that the blessing of God will manifest in financial prosperity: "Then the earth shall yield her increase; God, our own God, shall bless us" (verse 6). In a nation whose economy is based on agriculture, having the land yield its increase speaks of economic and financial blessing. This prayer is a harvest prayer for blessings.

The psalm then shifts from a prayer of petition to a prayer of decree: "God, our own God, shall bless us. God shall bless us" (verses 6–7). It seems that the psalmist's praise and thanksgiving moved him to shift from a petition for a blessing to a decree that God will surely bless His people.

Finally, the writer concludes that this blessing will cause the nations to fear Him: "God shall bless us, and all the ends of the earth shall fear Him" (Psalm 67:7). Thus the divine blessing will spread the fear of the Lord to people groups all over the globe.

What kind of blessings in your life will cause the nations—the world—to end up reverencing and fearing God? Right now, for the most part, unbelievers among the nations do not fear God on account of the blessing of God witnessed in His Church. What does such a blessing look like, that brings the nations to come to know Jesus, know His ways and, at the very least, fear and respect God and His people? *Extreme* blessings manifested in your life will bring all of this to pass. Get ready for His extreme blessings! The ten decrees in part 2 will help you see what this blessing looks like and, more importantly, walk out this blessing in your life.

7

The Power of Decrees

A decree is a command made in Jesus' name. It involves taking our authority in Christ and speaking forth God's Word in agreement with heaven's decrees. Jesus says in Matthew 16:19, "I will give you the keys of the kingdom of heaven, and whatever you bind on earth will be bound in heaven, and whatever you loose on earth will be loosed in heaven." The verb tense of "binding" and "loosing" in the Greek text actually reads, "What you bind on earth must be first bound in heaven and what you loose on earth must be first loosed in heaven." Leon Morris, in his excellent commentary on Matthew, says, "If we take this seriously, the Spirit-inspired church will be able to declare authoritatively what things are forbidden and what things are permitted."[1] God has the initiative. That is why so much of prayer means simply listening to God; in the moment we bind or loose what He wants us to bind or loose, the miracles of blessing take place.

Jesus did only what He saw His Father do and say (see John 5:19). Therefore He rarely made intercessory prayers; instead He made authoritative decrees like "Arise, take up your bed, and go to your house" (Matthew 9:6), "Stretch out your hand" (Mark 3:5) and "Lazarus, come forth!" (John 11:43). To the storm raging over the Sea of Galilee, He decreed, "Peace, be still!" Then "the wind ceased and there was a great calm" (Mark 4:39). Most of the miracles Jesus did came as a result of hearing from the Father and then decreeing that blessing.

Apostolic and prophetic decrees are powerful, but the Bible teaches that any words from our mouths can bless or curse:

> There is one who speaks like the piercings of a sword, but the tongue of the wise promotes health.
>
> Proverbs 12:18

> A wholesome tongue is a tree of life, but perverseness in it breaks the spirit.
>
> Proverbs 15:4

> Death and life are in the power of the tongue, and those who love it will eat its fruit.
>
> Proverbs 18:21

How many of us have said hurtful and destructive words, especially to our family members, that we later regret? Why? Because we essentially cursed them, even if we did not use an expletive. But the opposite is also true: When we speak God's Word and blessing over our lives and others, it can bring about transformation and even the miraculous.

True spoken blessing affirms the way God sees you and others. When you decree, you are prophesying the way you or someone or something is supposed to be, not how you are at the moment. When we bless someone, we are prophetically stating, "May Father God grant you all of His purposes for you; may God's full expectation for your life come to pass." And we know that God's intentions are to bless and prosper you: "'For I know the plans I have for you,' declares the LORD, 'plans to prosper you and not to harm you, plans to give you hope and a future'" (Jeremiah 29:11 NIV). This reveals the Father's heart toward us, His children.

Kings make decrees, and Jesus is the King of kings. But the Bible also says that we, God's children, are "kings and priests" (Revelation 1:6; 5:10). The Bible calls us a "royal priesthood" in 1 Peter 2:9, emphasizing that we are kings and ministers. This truth is very important. The book you are holding is designed to enable *you* to make the decrees that I am about to give you—to verbally, with conviction and faith, declare these blessings over your life and your loved ones. We *all* have authority to make decrees of blessing, as pastors over our congregations; as parents over our children; as relatives, friends and even strangers.

Apostolic Decrees

Though all believers in Jesus have authority to make decrees, the highest levels of decrees are apostolic decrees. Apostles are gifts to the Body of Christ. The Bible mentions this office more than any other office in the New Testament. The word *apostle* (or *apostles*) appears 74 times; the closest second would be all synonyms for *pastor* (such as elder, shepherd, overseer), at 67 times. In Ephesians 4:11–13, the apostle Paul writes,

> He Himself gave some to be apostles, some prophets, some evangelists, and some pastors and teachers, for the equipping of the saints for the work of ministry, for the edifying of the body of Christ, till we all come to the unity of the faith and of the knowledge of the Son of God, to a perfect man, to the measure of the stature of the fullness of Christ.

Clearly in this text we can see that apostles are for today. Until "we all come to the unity of the faith and of the knowledge of the Son of God, to a perfect man, to the measure of the stature of the fullness of Christ" (verse 12), we will need all five offices. I do not know any believer who would say that we have already "come to the unity of the faith" or become "a perfect man," nor have we attained the stature of Christ's fullness.

Furthermore, apostles serve as foundational gifts to the Church. I like the New Living Translation of Ephesians 2:19–20 (emphasis mine):

> You are members of God's family. Together, we are his house, built on the foundation of the *apostles* and the *prophets*. And the cornerstone is Christ Jesus himself.

Paul says that "God has appointed these in the church: first apostles, second prophets, third teachers" and so on (1 Corinthians 12:28); therefore I believe apostles have more spiritual authority than the others. God is the One who appoints and confers the measure of authority on an apostle. Not all apostles have the same measure, but the office of apostle, among those mentioned in Ephesians 4:11, carries the greater authority. My apostle, mentor and spiritual father, Peter Wagner, notes that "apostles have unusual authority"[2]; it is for advancing God's Kingdom, for enacting transformation of society and nations.

This authority is delegated by Jesus Himself:

> All authority has been given to Me in heaven and on earth. Go therefore and make disciples of all the nations, baptizing them in the name of the Father and of the Son and of the Holy Spirit, teaching them to observe all things that I have commanded you; and lo, I am with you always, even to the end of the age.

> Matthew 28:18–20

Having won back the authority lost in the Garden, Jesus gave that authority to His apostles, as well as to the whole Church, to fulfill the Great Commission.

The purpose of this authority is to serve God and others. "Whoever desires to become great among you," Jesus said, "let him be your servant" (Matthew 20:26). Abuse of authority is biblically illegal. Apostles must therefore be the ultimate servant-leaders.

I believe that God has called me to be an apostle. During 35-plus years of serving the Lord in vocational, ordained ministry, I have learned the power of apostolic decrees. When I make apostolic decrees based on the leading of the Holy Spirit, I have seen remarkable and miraculous breakthroughs.

I am saying this to build your faith, so that in reading the decrees out loud, you will believe that the blessing of God will manifest in your life. Keep in mind that I am declaring the Word of God over your life—not my words or the words of other people. The Bible says that His Word will not return empty and fruitless: "It is the same with my word. I send it out, and it always produces fruit. It will accomplish all I want it to, and it will prosper everywhere I send it" (Isaiah 55:11 NLT).

I experienced the power in an apostolic decree in June 2013, as I was hosting a roundtable of young leaders in HIM at our headquarters in Pasadena. Two of them, Greg and Rebecca Greenwood, live in Colorado Springs, and they received a phone call alerting them that they had to return and evacuate their home due to the spreading of a serious forest fire that had started the day before. Peter Wagner, who also lives in Colorado Springs, had already vacated an hour north to Denver. Before they rushed home, we prayed that both families' houses would be protected. As we were praying, I saw in my mind's eye a demarcation line protecting the homes. Sometimes God speaks to me through prophetic visions, and this was one of them. I saw the fire come right up to the line, but it did not cross it. So I made an apostolic decree as we were praying: "I see a demarcation line, and the fire will not cross that line. In Jesus' name I decree that the Wagner and Greenwood homes will be protected." Then we sent the Greenwoods back to Colorado Springs.

I found out a few days later that the fire came right up to the road that bordered the Wagners' and Greenwoods' houses. But it did not jump the road, and the homes were protected. Glory to God!

That week I flew to Seattle to speak at the Wagner Leadership Institute, a seminary started by Peter Wagner that I inherited in 2010. As international chancellor I was teaching and participating in the June graduation. The second day of lecturing (Friday, June 14), I received a phone call during the afternoon break from Cindy Jacobs, a well-known prophet and a dear friend. She called to tell me she believed I needed to make an apostolic decree that it would rain over Colorado Springs and that the firefighters would be able to put out the fire.

"Cindy, did you really hear from the Lord?" I asked. "Because there is no rain in the forecast." I had been tracking the fire very closely because of many friends I have in Colorado Springs.

Cindy replied, "I really do believe that you are to make that decree. I just called Peter Wagner, and I asked him to make a decree while he is in Denver." Even though I was not at home, I promised to bring her instruction to the church in Seattle and that we would pray.

That evening, the church stood in agreement as I made an apostolic decree that rain would come and put out the fire. Here is how quickly God answered the prayer decree: Late that Friday night and early Saturday morning, out of nowhere, rain came; it was sufficient for the firefighters to contain most of the fire. The next day *The Denver Post* reported that the cooler temperatures and rain helped the worn-out firefighters finally begin to turn back this highly destructive wildfire. "Cloud cover and the rain made a tremendous impact," Terry Maketa, sheriff of El Paso County, was quoted as saying. "We got our tails kicked for a couple of days . . . and today I think we delivered some blows."[3]

If this were an isolated incidence, you could say that it had nothing to do with apostolic decrees. But I have seen too many breakthroughs and miracles stemming from apostolic decrees that others and I have made to believe that this was purely coincidental. I want you to be in faith. As we look over the ten decrees of blessing, something will shift in your life, and you, too, can receive an amazing breakthrough of God's blessings.

PART II

The Ten Decrees
of Blessing

8

Decree #1: Love

I decree a blessing over you that God will grant you a Spirit of wisdom and revelation in the knowledge of God's love so that you can love and worship God and love others.

Called to Love

Bob Jones was a crusty, eccentric prophet. Many of his prophetic words were hard to understand, but one prophetic encounter that changed his life also changed my life forever. In 1975, Bob experienced extreme internal bleeding and had an out-of-body experience. His spirit left his body, and he found himself before the judgment seat of Christ. Jesus asked him one question: "Did you learn how to love?"

Bob was exposed. He could not lie; Jesus already knew his answer. He knew that he had not loved well during his short life as a believer on earth. Bob replied with deep sadness, "No."

Jesus responded, "You are not ready for heaven. Go and learn how to love." Immediately, Bob was back in his body as the doctors were feverishly operating on him. He survived the incident and made his quest in life to love well. I think he succeeded. He died at an old age almost forty years later, on Valentine's Day 2014, the day known for love.

When I was young, I wanted to know my divine calling, so I decided to go on a fast to hear from the Lord. I was hoping that God would call me to be the next Billy Graham. I so admire Mr. Graham to this day that he is in one of the few pictures on my desk: along with a picture of my parents and family is a picture of me with Billy Graham in his hotel room before the 2004 Billy Graham Crusade in Pasadena. During my fast, God surprised me by saying, "I have called you to a ministry of love." This shocked me. I knew it was God speaking because love was *not* on my radar. I was somewhat disappointed not to get the answer I was looking for. But now I see the wisdom behind this calling. As much as I enjoy preaching to crowds, sharing the Gospel and seeing souls come to Jesus, my ultimate goal is to love like Jesus loves. May it be yours as well.

Knowing the Destination

One of the hallmarks of humanity is its inexorable quest for knowledge. For thousands of years people have been collecting and sharing knowledge in the form of observations, discoveries, research and imaginations. As a people, we value education so much that we place our young people in school for their entire childhood and beyond. I am no different; my family will testify that I devour books and periodicals (not all Christian—think *Sports Illustrated*). But study and attainment of knowledge must have purpose—without a destination, the pursuit of knowledge can become a burdensome endeavor.

The writer of Ecclesiastes offered a warning against our desire for knowledge when he said, "There's no end to the publishing of books, and constant study wears you out so you're no good for anything else. The last and final word is this: Fear God. Do what he tells you" (Ecclesiastes 12:12–13 MESSAGE). Putting this final word into the context of the New Covenant, our call is to love God and love people—the greatest commandment. This can only be fulfilled in relationship.

Knowledge is meant to lead us to an encounter with the God of love. Jesus asked, "What good will it be for someone to gain the whole world, yet forfeit their soul?" (Matthew 16:26 NIV). When it comes to knowledge, Jesus might have said, "What good is it to know everything but still not enter into eternal joy and fulfillment?" Paul taught that even if we can understand all mysteries and all knowledge but do not have love, we are nothing (1 Corinthians 13:2).

The apostle John writes of this connection between knowing God and loving:

Everyone who loves is born of God and experiences a relationship with God. The person who refuses to love doesn't know the first thing about God, because God is love—so you can't know him if you don't love. . . . This is the kind of love we are talking about—not that we once upon a time loved God, but that he loved us and sent his Son as a sacrifice to clear away our sins and the damage they've done to our relationship with God.

1 John 4:7–8, 10 MESSAGE

The most important discovery in the universe is the knowledge of God. Whether we have truly understood this knowledge is demonstrated through our capacity to be loved and to love.

Growing up in the 1970s, I did not follow in the footsteps of my father, who was a minister. Instead, I rebelled and embraced the hippie culture of sex, drugs and rock 'n' roll. This lifestyle had its fun times, but I started to notice a growing emptiness in my soul.

While at a party one weekend, I felt jaded and frustrated because deep inside I knew there had to be more than I was experiencing. I went to a vacant room, and even though I did not believe in God, I found myself crying out to Him to reveal Himself to me. In that moment, I felt an incredible warmth and love envelop my body. Jesus was reaching out to me, and I was overwhelmed by how much He loved me.

I could not stop weeping for three days as waves of God's love crashed over me again and again. I have never been the same since that experience. To this day, I continue to be undone by the Lord's perfect love and seek to share His love with as many people as I can. I have committed my life to this call because there is no greater knowledge that can be shared than the knowledge of His love.

As Charles Wesley wrote in his famous lyrics, "Amazing love! How can it be, that Thou, my God, shouldst die for me?"

A Divine Knowing

God told the prophet Jeremiah, "Before I formed you in the womb I knew you, before you were born I set you apart; I appointed you as a prophet to the nations" (Jeremiah 1:5 NIV). The Hebrew word for "know" is *yada*, and it signifies a deep, personal knowing. The same term is used in Genesis 4:1 when Adam "knew" Eve and she conceived. God desires to know us intimately. There is also a yearning within people not just to know but to *be known*. Many believers have not experienced this type of knowing with the Lord. It requires more than just an intellectual understanding.

I can claim to know the president of the United States in that I know his name and the names of his family members. I know about his political, religious and moral views. But I do not really know the president. I have never spoken to him or spent time with him. Though I may know many things about him, I have no relationship with him. He does not know me. The same can be said for many believers when it comes to Jesus.

Some Christians pursue knowledge of God in devotions or quiet time that consists of reading the Bible. Now, I believe that the Bible is the infallible, inspired Word of God. (I like to tell my congregation that I believe in the whole Bible—including the maps!) But Bible reading can be either a mental exercise or a doorway to experiencing His presence. The Bible is not a biography but a love letter, written by our Savior to us. It is one of our main tools for learning about Jesus and His undying love.

Reading the Bible for knowledge does not guarantee an encounter with God. Jesus told the religious leaders, "You have your heads in your Bibles constantly because you think you'll find eternal life there. But you miss the forest for the trees. These Scriptures are all about me! And here I am, standing right before you" (John 5:39–40 MESSAGE). Bible scholars devote their lives to studying the Scriptures, but many of them do not know Jesus personally. Intellectual knowledge is not sufficient to have a relationship with the Lord. It requires a spiritual knowing.

The Holy Spirit Guide

The Bible is *information* that, when illuminated by the Holy Spirit, becomes *revelation* that leads to a divine encounter, which ultimately produces personal *transformation*. In order for Scriptures to become more than head knowledge, you must be willing to engage with the Holy Spirit. For that reason Paul says, "These things we also speak, not in words which man's wisdom teaches but *which the Holy Spirit teaches*, comparing spiritual things with spiritual" (1 Corinthians 2:13, emphasis mine). It is not enough to memorize verses, study theology or even perform miracles; at the end of the day, our intimacy with the Lord is what counts. Jesus illustrates this truth when He says many will come to Him, spouting spiritual résumés of prophecies, deliverances and signs and wonders, but His response will be, "I never *knew* you" (Matthew 7:23, emphasis mine).

We have received "not the spirit of the world, but the Spirit who is from God, that we might know the things that have been freely given to us by God" (1 Corinthians 2:12). The Holy Spirit was given to us to know God. He was sent to guide us into all truth and reveal the Truth, Jesus Christ (John 16:13). All the treasures of wisdom and knowledge are hidden in Christ (Colossians 2:2–3). My prayer, like Paul's, is that you may be filled with the knowledge of His will in all wisdom and spiritual understanding—that you may walk worthy of the Lord, fully pleasing Him, being fruitful in every good work and increasing in the knowledge of God through the power of the Holy Spirit (Colossians 1:9–10).

Knowledge Expressed through Love

The Spirit of wisdom and revelation is meant for us to know God better (Ephesians 1:17). It provides a grace and a pathway to intimacy. The Holy Spirit unlocks the door to the Father's throne so that we may sit on His lap and spend time with Him. It is one thing to know the construct of love but entirely different to *be in love*. People can describe love from an intellectual perspective but cannot fully understand it nor truly express it unless they are in a love relationship.

One of my spiritual children has a nine-year-old son named Isaac. When Isaac was younger, his father would sing to him before it was time to sleep. One of the songs Isaac loved to hear was "Oh, How I Love Jesus" (by Frederick Whitfield). Occasionally, his father would switch the lyrics to include his son's name. Lying in bed with Isaac, he would sing,

> Oh, how I love Isaac,
> Oh, how I love Isaac,
> Oh, how I love Isaac because he is my son.

Isaac would ask his dad to sing it over and over. One particular night as the father finished the serenade, through the still silence of darkness arose a tiny voice:

> Oh, how I love Daddy,
> Oh, how I love Daddy,
> Oh, how I love Daddy because he is my dad.

What a beautiful picture of knowing the Father and responding in love. To know God means to hear and receive His overwhelming heart of love for us and echo that same affection back to Him; we love because He first loved us (1 John 4:19). Is it possible that many songs we sing in worship are childlike imitations of the lullabies He sings over us?

The way I measure love is by the way I love my wife and children. Am I being kind, patient, gracious, encouraging, attentive, generous and sacrificing? Jesus took it to a new level when He challenged us to love our enemies (Matthew 5:44). A good gauge of the heart is not just to ask ourselves how well we love those close to us but also our enemies or those who do not treat us well. People can usually love others who love them back, but it takes a supernatural grace to love people when they have hurt you.

Love Expressed through Grace

In 1984, 22-year-old Jennifer Thompson was raped when a man broke into her home and held a knife to her throat. After the attack, Jennifer went to the police and identified her perpetrator from a photo; later, she singled the same man, Ronald Cotton, out of a lineup. Based on Jennifer's testimony, Cotton was convicted and sentenced to life in prison at age 22. Jennifer hated Ronald with all her heart and was relieved that justice was served.

Cotton, however, appealed and was retried in 1987. An inmate named Bobby Poole in the same prison as Cotton confessed to his cellmate that he was actually Jennifer's assailant. When they brought Bobby to court, Jennifer testified that she had never seen him before. Blinded by her rage, she wanted only to see Cotton suffer and die. Based on Jennifer's testimony, the court convicted Cotton again and added another life sentence.

Ronald Cotton still insisted on his innocence. His break came in 1995 when he was watching the O.J. Simpson trial on television and learned about DNA evidence, which he had never heard of. He contacted his lawyer, and evidence from his case was tested for DNA. The results conclusively showed Ronald Cotton had not raped Jennifer Thompson; Bobby Poole was the attacker. After eleven long years, Ronald was cleared of all charges and became the first person exonerated using DNA evidence in North Carolina.

Jennifer Thompson and Ronald Cotton met for the first time two years later. Jennifer was devastated; for over a decade, she had been a victim, but now she felt like an offender. Jennifer could not even stand at their meeting and sobbed uncontrollably. "If I spent every minute of every hour of every day for the rest of my life telling you that I'm sorry," she asked, "can you ever forgive me?"

Ronald did something she had never imagined: Weeping, he said, "Jennifer, I forgave you years ago."

Thirteen years after her attack, Jennifer was no longer angry. Sitting in front of Ronald was like "literally looking at grace and mercy." In the years since they have become friends, even writing a book together entitled *Picking Cotton: Our Memoir of Injustice and Redemption.* They travel the nation sharing their amazing story. Jennifer was even able to forgive her rapist, Bobby Poole, saying, "I forgave Bobby Poole because I watched Ronald forgive me."[1]

Love Never Fails

Jennifer and Ronald's testimony of forgiveness and restoration is a reflection of the Father's grace to the world. Paul declares, "God demonstrates His own love toward us, in that while we were still sinners, Christ died for us" (Romans 5:8). He modeled true love by reconciling us back to God and giving us the ministry of reconciliation (2 Corinthians 5:18). We are now ambassadors of His love, administering grace to the broken and hurting. *To know this loving God and to make Him known*—this is our purpose. This is our call.

Now, make this declaration over yourself:

> *I decree a blessing over myself that God will give me a Spirit of wisdom and revelation in the knowledge of God's love so that I can love and worship God and love others.*

9

Decree #2: The Grace of God

I decree a blessing over you that you will grow in the grace of God and be a person of grace and truth, and that His grace will give you the power and favor to fulfill your destiny.

Grace Means Power

The word *grace*, or *charis* in Greek, appears 155 times in the New Testament. Its traditional definition is the undeserved favor of God, and while this is correct, grace is also the power of God to transform. Recently, I celebrated my 41st year following Jesus, and that is a true testimony of how amazing God's grace is. When I was fifteen, I started using drugs. I am not talking about dabbling in marijuana; I was doing everything I could get my hands on—cocaine, LSD, speed, barbiturates and heroin. I was out of control. I was thrown in jail at fifteen and suspended from high school at sixteen; by the ripe old age of seventeen, I was a drug addict and pusher selling more than $2,000 per month to support my habit. On top of this, I dropped out of high school, the unpardonable sin in an Asian family. *Why bother?* I thought. *I'm dumb anyway.* I was a mess and totally lost.

I really believe I was one of the most rebellious, deceived and selfish people in the world. So my encounter with Jesus and His love in May 1973—at a drug party!—was nothing less than transformational. My conscience was awakened, I was born again and, without anyone telling me to do so, I got a haircut—which shocked my dad. More importantly, I gave up and renounced drugs. At a Deep Purple concert on May 29, 1973, I threw my drugs onto the floor of the Baltimore Civic Center, walked out of the concert and made a decision to follow and obey God. To this day, I have never backslid or returned to drugs. That is the grace of God—the power to transform. The Bible describes how this grace can change your life:

> God can point to us in all future ages as examples of the incredible wealth of his grace and kindness toward us, as shown in all he has done for us who are united with Christ Jesus. God saved you by his grace when you believed. And you can't take credit for this; it is a gift from God. Salvation

is not a reward for the good things we have done, so none of us can boast about it. For we are God's masterpiece.

Ephesians 2:7–10 NLT

You are His masterpiece. He offers grace to save you, transform you and fulfill your destiny in Him because of His great love for you. He wants to *lavish* you with His grace.

You do not have to be a slave to sin or have addictions in your life. If God can transform me, He can change your life. Grace gives you the power to say no to sin. "For the grace of God has appeared, bringing salvation for all people, training us to renounce ungodliness and worldly passions, and to live self-controlled, upright, and godly lives in the present age" (Titus 2:11–12 ESV). God's will for you is to walk in victory and have total freedom in your life. He wants to bless you with His grace.

Grace to Fulfill Your Destiny

Grace is power not only for transformation but for you to fulfill your God-given destiny. Jeremiah was called even before his birth: "I knew you before I formed you in your mother's womb. Before you were born I set you apart and appointed you as my prophet to the nations" (Jeremiah 1:5 NLT). To those who submit to God's calling, He gives grace to fulfill that purpose in life.

We see how God gave grace and power to advance His Kingdom through His apostles in the book of Acts (see Acts 6:8; 11:23; 14:26; 15:40; 18:27). *God's grace is upon you, too,* and He has called you to do great things for Him. But when you achieve anything for Him, you will give Him the glory because you will know that anything you have accomplished is by the grace of God. You will be able to say along with Paul, "But by the grace of God I am what I am, and His grace toward me was not in vain; but I labored more abundantly than they all, yet not I, but the grace of God which was with me" (1 Corinthians 15:10).

God has called you to be the head and not the tail (Deuteronomy 28:13); He has called you to be successful. He will give you the grace to do what He has called you to do in life. For me to go from being a high school dropout to having two graduate degrees from one of the top seminaries in the world is absolutely the grace of God. When I dropped out of high school, I could hardly read, write or spell; now this book will be the fourteenth I have published. This could only be done by His grace.

I believe *you* will do even better. Someone reading this will become a bestselling author; another will be a top doctor, or a scientist, lawyer, director, educator or successful businessperson. Whatever you are dreaming of becoming, the grace of God will help you get there.

The Favor of God

Grace is God's favor over your life. When the angel Gabriel announced to Mary, "Rejoice, highly favored one, the Lord is with you" (Luke 1:28), the word used for "favor" is the same Greek word for grace, *charis*. Though Mary has a special place in salvation history, because of what Jesus did for us through His death and resurrection, we, too, are highly favored of God. Jesus decreed this favor in His inaugural address at the local synagogue, when He opened the scroll to Isaiah 61 and proclaimed,

> The Spirit of the LORD is upon me, for he has anointed me to bring Good News to the poor. He has sent me to proclaim that captives will be released, that the blind will see, that the oppressed will be set free, and that *the time of the LORD's favor* has come.

> Luke 4:18 NLT, emphasis mine

If space allowed I could enumerate many, many testimonies of God's favor in my life; at the very least I have to tell you how I met Billy Graham. As I shared, Dr. Graham is my hero. Over the years I have attended Billy Graham leadership conferences, hoping to meet him, but I never got close. When he did a crusade at the famous Pasadena Rose Bowl Stadium, however, I was invited to join the executive committee of key pastors in Los Angeles. When the forty of us met with the director of the Billy Graham Crusade, I asked if we would be meeting Dr. Graham. "I am so sorry," he replied. "In the past, you would have met with him, but because of his failing health [he had broken his hip the year before] and his age, Billy Graham will not be meeting with the executive committee." He also explained that, contrary to tradition, members of the executive committee would not take turns sitting on the platform. Bummer! I gave the situation to the Lord.

Two days before the crusade began, I received a phone call from the executive director. "Dr. Graham would like to meet with a handful of pastors," he told me, "and you have been selected with four others. Can you meet this Tuesday at 3:00 p.m.?"

Are you kidding me? I shook off the disbelief. "I'll be there!"

The meeting was surreal. Dr. Jack Hayford, Dr. Lloyd Ogilvie, Bishop Ken Ulmer and a Hispanic pastor whose name I forgot joined me in Dr. Graham's hotel room. I guess I was their token Asian! I asked if Dr. Graham would lay hands on us and impart his gift of evangelism. In his humble, inimitable way, he said, "First I want you men to lay hands on me and impart to me what you have, and then I will lay hands on you and pray for you."

When the crusade began, I was again asked to join Dr. Hayford, Dr. Ogilvie and Bishop Ulmer in laying hands on and praying for Dr. Graham in his on-site trailer. Did I mention that it was surreal? Who was I to lay hands on Billy Graham before he got up to speak each night? In the end, they asked me to sit on the platform the last night of the conference.

This may not seem like a big deal, but it was for me. The takeaway from the story is that God wants to give you the desires of your heart (Psalm 37:4). What do you want God to do for *you*? Decree favor over your life, for His favor is upon you. It may not happen right away, but in His perfect time your desires will be fulfilled.

How to Receive More Grace

How can you consistently experience God's grace and favor in your life? One amazing thing about grace is that you can grow in it: "But grow in the grace and knowledge of our Lord and Savior Jesus Christ" (2 Peter 3:18). The answer to receiving and growing in grace is found in one word: humility. Many value humility without knowing how to walk in it.

The simple key to walking in humility is choosing to be humble. Commenting on 1 Peter 5:5, "Be clothed with humility," Peter Wagner says,

> This is an interesting metaphor. Being humble is, apparently, like getting dressed. Who puts your clothes on each morning? You do! You are not naked at this moment because you decided to put clothes on and you dressed yourself. In the same way, we all are supposed to be clothed with humility. It is the active verb again. We must decide to do it, and then do it! . . . "Whoever exalts himself will be humbled, and he who humbles himself will be exalted" (Matthew 23:12).

This quote from Jesus is built around action verbs. What you finally achieve in your life will clearly depend on the decisions you make now, and the actions you take to implement those decisions. Jesus would not have put it this way unless He knew that you personally had the power to decide to humble yourself or to exalt yourself. [1]

What changed my life was getting honest and humble before God. When I cried out to God at my friend's party, I said honestly, "God, I don't know if You exist. But if You do exist and there is a heaven and a hell, reveal Your truth to me." In that moment, I humbled myself before God for the first time; He saw my heart and poured out His grace. I was like the Prodigal Son in Luke 15:17–19 (NLT):

> When he finally came to his senses, he said to himself, "At home even the hired servants have food enough to spare, and here I am dying of hunger! I will go home to my father and say, 'Father, I have sinned against both heaven and you, and I am no longer worthy of being called your son. Please take me on as a hired servant.'"

This proud young man first "came to his senses" and then humbled himself to repent before God and his father.

Today, I make a choice to humble myself daily, for "God opposes the proud but favors the humble" (James 4:6 NLT). I do not want God to oppose me—I want His favor. One choice I make is to give glory to God for all the blessings in my life and for anything that goes well. I simply pray silently, *Lord, I thank You for the blessings in my life.* More specifically I might say, *I thank You for my new grandchildren in my daughter's womb. I thank You for healthy, happy, full-term babies.* Or, *Thank You for the doctor's report that I am totally healthy.* You can fill in the blank with your life's victories and give Him all the praise and glory.

If someone compliments me, I try to deflect praise. People sometimes tell me how great my adult kids are, and my response is often, "It's because they have a great mom." First of all, this statement is true; it also gives me a practical opportunity to humble myself before God.

I love sports, and when I see the star player for the winning college team giving credit to the coaches and other teammates, I say to myself, *That kid is going to go far.* Favor will follow those who humble themselves. Choose humility and you will see the grace of God magnified in your life—big time.

Now decree this over your life out loud:

> *I decree a blessing over myself that I will grow in the grace of God and be a person of grace and truth, and that His grace will give me the power and favor to fulfill my destiny.*

10

Decree #3: The Power of the Holy Spirit

I decree a blessing over you that you will be full of the power of the Holy Spirit, be activated in the gifts of the Spirit and shift the spiritual atmosphere by His holy presence wherever you go.

Receiving the Power

Imagine you are one of Jesus' twelve disciples. You have experienced more than three years of intimate fellowship with Him, living with Him, hearing outstanding teachings and witnessing one miracle after another. Suddenly, He hits you with the news that He is leaving the earth and tells you that you will be better off if He goes. The Jewish people have been praying for the long-awaited Messiah for more than a millennium, and now that He is here, He says He is about to leave. Would you not ask, "What the heck is He talking about?"

This is exactly what Jesus told His disciples.

> Because I have said [I am going away], sorrow has filled your heart. Nevertheless I tell you the truth. It is to your advantage that I go away; for if I do not go away, the Helper will not come to you; but if I depart, I will send Him to you. And when He has come, He will convict the world of sin, and of righteousness, and of judgment.
>
> John 16:6–8

It is "to your advantage" that Jesus returned to His Father because you need the Holy Spirit to be your Helper! The Holy Spirit, the third Person of the Trinity and God Himself, is the greatest gift to the Church next to the gift of salvation. We often say at HRock Church, "The presence of the Holy Spirit is not just the icing on the cake—it is the cake!"

There is no question that, if you are born again, you have the Holy Spirit (see Romans 8:9). But what I am talking about is the power of the Holy Spirit that Jesus promised all believers in Acts 1:8: "But you shall receive power when the Holy Spirit has come upon you; and you shall be witnesses to Me in Jerusalem, and in all Judea and Samaria, and to the end of the earth."

Have you noticed that many of the great men and women of God in Church history could point to a distinct experience of receiving the power of God? And that this experience catapulted each of them into greater effectiveness and fruitfulness? This experience has been described in many different terms—a "baptism in the Holy Spirit," the "gift of the Holy Spirit," being "filled with the Holy Spirit." Regardless of terminology, they received the same thing: the power of the Holy Spirit.

I emphasize a *distinct* experience because it usually happens at a time distinct from a person's conversion. It could happen simultaneously (see Acts 10), but testimonies usually indicate that this type of encounter with the Holy Spirit is subsequent to and distinct from one's conversion.

I received the power of the Holy Spirit in 1974, in a small congregation near Niagara Falls, New York. I write about the encounter in my book *Spirit-Led Evangelism*:

> Our youth group from The Church of Atonement got up to sing before their congregation. We then sang the song "Day by Day" from the musical *Godspell*. . . . I remember singing the words "To see thee more clearly, to love thee more dearly and to follow thee more nearly . . . day by day. . . ." Yes, that's my prayer to God. I didn't just sing these words—I really prayed them and meant the prayer with all my heart.
>
> "God, I really want see you more clearly. I really want to love you more dearly. And God, I really want to follow you more nearly, day by day."

As I began to worship the Lord with these words, tears began to stream down my face. I sensed the deep love of God and the awesome presence of God. Then, this remarkable tingling, electrifying sensation started to spread throughout my feet, up my legs, up to my head, through my arms and down to my fingers. The sensation was so intense that my fingers could not move. . . . The numbing vibrations continued to increase and my tears of worship turned to sobs of joy. I knew God was touching me.

To say the least, I was making quite a scene to the point that the youth leader in charge had to come up to me and ask me to leave the room. I went to the men's room at his suggestion. I continued to weep and worship in the bathroom. I sensed that God was anointing me for a purpose. I didn't hear an audible voice or see anything, but I knew in my heart that God had heard my prayer of dedication and service. And, that He was empowering me for that service.[1]

It is important not to compare your encounters with the Holy Spirit with other people's encounters. Each one is different but powerful. Jesus received the Holy Spirit very gently as it descended on Him like a dove (Matthew 3:16), but the Holy Spirit came upon the disciples with extraordinary manifestations (Acts 2:2–4). To each, the same Holy Spirit brought different encounters.

The beautiful thing about the Holy Spirit is that God wants you to be filled often. "There is one baptism of the Holy Spirit," I have said, "but there are many fillings with the same Holy Spirit." The Bible says in Ephesians 5:18 (NLT), "Don't be drunk with wine, because that will ruin your life. Instead, be filled with the Holy Spirit." The Greek word for "filled" is in the continuous present tense, making the verse truly read, "*Be continually filled* with the Holy Spirit." We see this happening in the early Church some time after the believers were filled with the Holy Spirit. "And when they had prayed, the place where they were assembled together was shaken; and they were all filled with the Holy Spirit, and they spoke the word of God with boldness" (Acts 4:31). Even if you were filled with the Spirit before, why not receive more right now?

I declare that God wants you to have the power of the Holy Spirit, which will help you be more of an effective, victorious Christian. It will help you be a blessing to those who do not know Jesus. By faith, receive the power and fresh infilling of the Holy Spirit.

A Life of Being Filled

Here is how I stay continually filled with the Holy Spirit:

1. I daily choose to walk in obedience to God. The Bible says the Holy Spirit is "given to those who obey Him" (Acts 5:32). Jesus said if anyone wants to be His disciple, "let him deny himself, take up his cross daily, and follow Me" (Luke 9:23). This is a heart attitude; daily

I offer to Him my life "as a living sacrifice, holy and pleasing to God" (Romans 12:1 NIV)—it is my spiritual act of worship.

2. Every day, usually in the morning, and often throughout the day, I ask the Father to fill me with the Holy Spirit. If I need to drink plenty of water on a daily basis to be healthy, how much more should I drink of the Holy Spirit by asking Him to fill me so I can stay spiritually sharp and healthy? Luke 11:13 says, "If you then, being evil, know how to give good gifts to your children, how much more will your heavenly Father give the Holy Spirit to those who ask Him!" I ask Him in faith to fill me, and by faith I receive that infilling. This is not rocket science; if we do not have, it is because we do not ask (see James 4:2).

3. I keep before me the vision of a great revival and harvest. What this does is give me a holy dissatisfaction with the status quo. It keeps me hungry for more. "Blessed are those who hunger and thirst for righteousness," Jesus said, "for they shall be filled" (Matthew 5:6).

4. Finally, I try to receive an impartation from others who are anointed and full of the Holy Spirit. I am a God chaser, and those whom He has anointed carry His glory. You may find such people around you; they could be your pastors or anointed, godly people in your church or city. If you are really hungry, you may want to

visit another church, city or nation where a move of God is taking place—for example, by making a "pilgrimage" to one of the global hot spots where God is moving in revival: China, India, Africa, Brazil and Indonesia. Our network, HIM, leads short-term mission trips to these five hot spots to do ministry, but our primary goal is to receive an impartation through the revivals. (For short-term ministry trip opportunities, check out our website, harvestim.org.)

The Purpose of Spiritual Gifts

God loves to give, and He has given spiritual gifts—not just to His whole Body but to *you* specifically:

> In his grace, God has given us different gifts for doing certain things well. So if God has given you the ability to prophesy, speak out with as much faith as God has given you. If your gift is serving others, serve them well. If you are a teacher, teach well. If your gift is to encourage others, be encouraging. If it is giving, give generously. If God has given you leadership ability, take the responsibility seriously. And if you have a gift for showing kindness to others, do it gladly.
>
> Romans 12:6–8 NLT

The power and gifts of the Holy Spirit are given to you so that you can be a blessing to others, as we also read in

Ephesians 4:11 and 1 Corinthians 12:1–11. In order to bless others, the gifts need to be activated and employed. The key to fulfilling your destiny is to discover your gifts and employ them for Kingdom purposes. I highly recommend Peter Wagner's bestselling book *Finding Your Spiritual Gifts*.[2] It includes a spiritual gifts test at the end to help you discover your gifts.

You also are carriers of God's glory; Paul writes of "Christ in you, the hope of glory" (Colossians 1:27). You carry the presence of God with you wherever you go. When you are filled with and full of the Holy Spirit more and more, that is when miracles begin to happen. That is when you become a blessing to others.

Have you ever gone into an empty restaurant to find people streaming in because you bring the presence of God? Charles Finney could walk through a factory in Rochester, New York, without saying a word, and people would start to weep because the presence of God was released through him. God wants us to be so filled with His presence that we "leak" onto others, for when you bring God's presence, you are bringing God's blessings.

Kevin Dedmon shares a wonderful testimony of his son, Chad, who went to the Houston Astrodome to serve people devastated by Hurricane Katrina:

> On one occasion, Chad was praying for a woman on a cot. As he was releasing God's presence to her, a man who was

walking by shouted out, "What in the —— did you do to me?" Chad looked up toward the startled man and assured him that he had not done anything. The man shot back, "Yes, you did! As I was walking past you, my knee felt like it was on fire! What did you do?" After further inquiry, the man explained that he had had a knee injury that debilitated him for years. As he was limping past Chad, the fire hit him in his knee, and he was completely healed. Chad explained that the power of God must have leaked onto the man as Chad was praying for the woman. The man received Jesus on the spot and left very happy![3]

May God so fill you with His Spirit that you "leak" His presence and blessing to those around you! Now let's say this decree aloud:

> *I decree a blessing over myself that I will be continually full of the power of the Holy Spirit, be activated in the gifts of the Spirit and shift the spiritual atmosphere by His holy presence wherever I go.*

11

Decree #4: Identity

I decree a blessing over you that you will know who you are in Christ: that you are the righteousness of God in Christ; that you are God's friend, God's child; and that as His Bride, you are called to reign in life together with Jesus forever.

Words Imprinted

"You are a stupid boy!" These words crushed my spirit and left an indelible imprint on my soul until I was seventeen. I was only five when they were spoken. They did not come from my father but from my first-grade teacher.

I had emigrated from Korea less than a year before. On perhaps the second day of first grade, the teacher was showing us how to write the alphabet. She drew a large letter *A* on her blackboard and instructed us to write exactly as she had over two lines on the pieces of paper before us. I did not hear "over the two lines"; I only heard, "Write exactly like me." Desiring to obey and please her, I did what I perceived she was asking for; I drew a big *A* that filled the whole page, around the size of my teacher's *A*. As checked the first graders' papers, she nodded and said, "That's good," to the other students. But when she came to my paper, her voice rose emotionally. "No, no, this is wrong! You are a stupid boy!" That destructive statement imprinted an identity in me, which lasted until I gave my life to Jesus at the age of seventeen. (By the way, I forgave her a long time ago.)

Through my elementary years and up to high school, I never studied or tried in school. I got by with Cs and some Bs. I did a lot of cheating. *Why bother?* I said to myself. *I'm not as smart as the others. I'm a stupid boy.* Now, I'm not totally blaming my performance on what my first-grade teacher said; but it is amazing how "decrees" can positively impact your life or absolutely devastate it.

But God says you have the mind of Christ (1 Corinthians 2:16), and that Christ Jesus has become wisdom for you from God (1 Corinthians 1:30). After my conversion, I started getting straight As in college (a real testimony of the transforming work of His grace), and I went on to get my master's and doctorate at Fuller Theological Seminary with a 4.0 average. I know deep inside I have the mind of Christ, that He has become my wisdom, that I am smart and that

I am even good looking! Go ahead and renounce the negative words spoken over your life: "You will never amount to anything," "You don't have the brains (or looks) to make it in life," and so on.

Your Identity Determines Your Destiny

Who am I? Although many have attempted to answer this fundamental query, we can only truly know who we are by knowing who God is. Abba God reproduces Himself. God is love, and He created us in love, for love and to love. Our identity can never be understood separate from the love of God. This is why the greatest commandments are to love God and to love people. The essence of love is who God is, and it is who we are.

That being said, everybody's encounter with the God of love is unique. People experience different aspects and degrees of love depending on one of five stages of identity in the Lord: (1) sinner, or slave to sin, (2) servant, or slave to righteousness, (3) friend, (4) son, (5) bride.

We must understand these steps in our spiritual development. Your relationship with God will look very different as a son compared to a friend or as a bride compared to a servant. The apostolic decree of identity is meant to mature you into the fullness of your identity. Where are you in your journey with the Lord?

Stage 1: Sinner/Slave to Sin

The pinnacle of God's creation was man, the only being He made in His own image. Though God was a father to Adam and Eve, from the moment they disobeyed God, people were born under the curse of sin, separated from God and destined to die. "Adam sinned, and that sin brought death into the world. Now everyone has sinned, and so everyone must die" (Romans 5:12 CEV).

David recognized the reality of our fallen nature when he wrote, "Surely I was sinful at birth, sinful from the time my mother conceived me" (Psalm 51:5 NIV). And Jesus said that everyone who sins is a slave to sin (John 8:34). The first stage of our spiritual identity, therefore, is that of a sinner, a slave to sin with Satan as our master. Our poor choices have alienated us from God and made us His enemies (Colossians 1:21).

Stage 2: Servant/Slave to Righteousness

There is no earthly or human solution to our sin problem. We are completely unable to change our nature. No amount of repentance, meditation, ritual cleansing, good works or sacrifice will free us from our bondage to sin. This is why Paul exclaims, "O wretched man that I am! Who will deliver me from this body of death?" (Romans 7:24). But the solution is presented in the very next verse: "Thanks be to God, who delivers me through Jesus Christ our Lord!" (Romans 7:25 NIV).

God has provided a way for us to be transformed into a new creature through Christ. If we have made Jesus the Lord of our lives, our sin is forgiven and we have become a new creation. The sinful nature is crucified and we have a new nature. No longer slaves to sin, we become slaves of righteousness (Romans 6:17–18). It is not necessarily bad to be a slave; it just depends on who your master is.

This stage marks the transformation from "sinner" to "saint." Like a hairy caterpillar bound to the dirt that changes into a beautiful butterfly fluttering free in the sky, our metamorphosis into a saint is a radical conversion that transforms our fundamental identity. The Greek term for "saint" is the same word used to describe God's very own Spirit (*hagios*).

Throughout the New Testament, believers are referred to as "saints" (see Romans 1:7; 8:27; 12:13; 15:26; 1 Corinthians 1:2; Ephesians 1:1; 2:19; Philippians 1:1). Many Christians still believe they are sinners saved by grace, but this is a past reality. We were *once* sinners saved by grace, but *now* we are saints living by the Spirit. Not only are we saints, we are also a royal priesthood (1 Peter 2:9), the Body of Christ (1 Corinthians 12:27) and a temple of the Holy Spirit (1 Corinthians 6:19)!

Paul proclaims this good news over and over again in his writings:

> Therefore, if anyone is in Christ, he is a new creation; old things have passed away; behold, all things have become new.
>
> 2 Corinthians 5:17

I have been crucified with Christ; it is no longer I who live, but Christ lives in me.

Galatians 2:20

Those who belong to Christ Jesus have crucified the flesh with its passions and desires.

Galatians 5:24 NIV

Serving the Lord is a privilege and honor. Christ did not die on the cross simply to get servants, however. He has plenty of those: They are called angels. He gave His life to set people free *for a purpose*—we were meant to be more than just servants to a divine Master.

Stage 3: Friends

The disciples understood that Jesus was their master. They addressed Him as such and left everything to serve and follow Him. After almost three years together, Jesus delivered a stunning message to this ragtag group:

Greater love has no one than this, than to lay down one's life for his friends. You are My friends if you do whatever I command you. No longer do I call you servants, for a servant does not know what his master is doing; but I have called you friends, for all things that I heard from My Father I have made known to you.

John 15:13–15

The disciples were given a divine promotion. The King of kings and Lord of lords no longer regarded them as servants but was inviting them to be friends. This dramatically shifted not only how they viewed themselves but also how they related to the Lord. Servants work to please the master, often laboring with a component of fear; they work for favor and reward or the avoidance of punishment. Friends do not work to please each other; they simply find joy in each other's presence and are willing to serve out of love, not fear. Jesus even described the love of a friend as willing to sacrifice one's life for another.

You are God's friends. As friends, we still serve the Lord in all we do, but our mentality has shifted. You can be a servant to someone without being a friend, but you cannot be a true friend without being willing to serve. A servant can even love and honor his master, but it is very different from the love of a friend. Jesus, the ultimate Friend, lays down His life for His sheep (John 10:11).

Could your relationship with God be characterized as that of a servant to a master, or are you His friend? It is possible to talk to the Lord like Moses, face-to-face, as one speaks to a friend (Exodus 33:11). As wonderful as this friendship is, there are levels of even greater intimacy with the Lord.

Stage 4: Sons and Daughters

At the end of the day, friends go back to their own homes (hopefully). Sometimes you have to kick them out. But children stay with their father. Children are closer to the father than friends and servants are. Jesus says slaves have no permanent place in the family, but a son belongs to it forever (John 8:35).

Children see a different side of the father than friends do. Children even look like their dad. They have special access, significance and favor. They receive an inheritance. They are nurtured from infancy to maturity. They are snuggled, played with, tickled, hugged, kissed and lavished with love. I treat my children very differently than I do my friends. I do not snuggle with my friends (anymore!).

The Bible loudly declares our place as children in the family of God:

> For you did not receive the spirit of bondage again to fear, but you received the Spirit of adoption by whom we cry out, "Abba, Father." The Spirit Himself bears witness with our spirit that we are children of God, and if children, then heirs—heirs of God and joint heirs with Christ, if indeed we suffer with Him, that we may also be glorified together.
>
> Romans 8:15–17

> Because you are sons, God has sent forth the Spirit of His Son into your hearts, crying out, "Abba, Father!" Therefore you are no longer a slave but a son, and if a son, then an heir of God through Christ.
>
> Galatians 4:6–7

See what great love the Father has lavished on us, that we should be called children of God! And that is what we are!

1 John 3:1 NIV

It is important to note that we become children of God as soon as we accept Jesus as Lord and Savior. Just because we are adopted into His family, however, does not mean we see ourselves as a child or relate to God as a Father. That only comes through faith and experience. Many believers have difficulty addressing the Lord as Father, but it is not only possible to do so, it is God's desire. Jesus says, "Truly I tell you, unless you change and become like children, you will never enter the kingdom of heaven" (Matthew 18:3 NRSV). Become like a child before the Lord. He is the best Dad in the whole world. Give Him a chance to prove it.

Even with the benefits of being a child of God, there is an higher level in our spiritual maturity that can only be experienced at the final stage of our identity.

Stage 5: Beloved Bride of Christ

Raising kids is one of the greatest joys in life. But in the end, children grow up and leave the house (once again, hopefully—and sometimes accompanied by a loving kick). Though a child becomes an adult and moves out, our spouses stay with us no matter what. Marriage is the most intimate relationship a human being can have with another person.

There are things that I tell my wife that I do not tell my kids or my friends. Certain things are reserved only for marriage, which means becoming one flesh—a great mystery. "'For this reason a man will leave his father and mother and be united to his wife, and the two will become one flesh.' This is a profound mystery—but I am talking about Christ and the church" (Ephesians 5:31–32 NIV).

Earthly marriage is a symbol of our ultimate spiritual relationship with Jesus, which Paul understood well. "I am jealous for you with a godly jealousy," he wrote the Corinthians. "I promised you to one husband, to Christ, so that I might present you as a pure virgin to him" (2 Corinthians 11:2 NIV). The rest of Scripture confirms this understanding: The entire book of Song of Songs, for example, is no mere human love story; it presents a prophetic picture of Jesus and the Church. Isaiah 54:5–7, Hosea 2:19 and Revelation 19:7 also allude to this marital relationship. Why would God create the institution of marriage if people were not able to experience that same level of intimacy with Him? This may be a difficult and even offensive concept to some, but it makes perfect and beautiful sense in the Kingdom.

Even if you are not ready for this level of intimacy with the Lord, know that this is our destiny. It would be inappropriate for an eight-year-old to desire and plan for marriage, but it *is* important for this child's mother and father to love each other and model a healthy marriage. Get connected with believers who have cultivated an intimate relationship with

Jesus as a bride would to a groom. Maturity was always meant to occur within the context of family.

Moving On Up

If you find yourself in one of the first four stages, be encouraged. The Lord is extending a divine hand of invitation to come up to the next level. All that is required is for you to respond in faith and start embracing the mindset of a friend, son or bride. We never leave the heart of the previous stage (except for that of slave to sin); each level builds upon itself to create an exquisite depth to our relationship with God. My wife is my best friend and serves me better than anyone else in my life. May that be true of us with our Lord Jesus.

Creation is groaning for the sons of God to be revealed (Romans 8:19–23). If you activate your clairaudience, your spiritual ears, you can detect a deep hum emanating from the earth. It is a repetitive refrain echoing over the land and seas directed to the people of God. Silence your heart and listen for a moment. Our planet is pleading:

> Know who you are.
> Embrace your royal identity.
> Come into your destiny.
> We are waiting. We are waiting!

Declare this decree with faith and conviction over your life:

I decree a blessing over myself that I will know who I am in Christ: that I am the righteousness of God in Christ; that I am God's friend, God's child; and that as His Bride, I am called to reign in life together with Jesus forever.

12

Decree #5: Christlike Character

I decree a blessing over you that you will be transformed from glory to glory into the image and character of Christ, growing and demonstrating the fruit of the Holy Spirit.

What Does Christlike Character Look Like?

God loves you just the way you are, but because He loves you, He does not want you to stay as you are—He wants you to grow and be conformed into the image of Christ. That is your destiny. From the beginning God has preordained for Himself a family that will reflect the image of His Son, Jesus. "Whom He foreknew, He also predestined to be conformed to the image of His Son, that He might be the firstborn among many brethren" (Romans 8:29).

What does Christlike character look like? For me, it can be summed up in one word, *love*. We have already considered God's love in chapter 8, but because love is so important to walking out His blessings, let's look further into this important subject. The Bible does not use the term *love* as loosely as we do; we "love" pizza, football, fill in the blank, yet we use the same word to express our love for God and for our families. The Greeks helped us understand the depths of love by giving us four words to express it. The first, *phileo*, refers to friendship or brotherly love, as in 2 Peter 1:7. Next, *eros*—which is not found in the New Testament—is used for sexual love; it is how we get the word "erotic." *Storge*, the third, has to do with family love (see Romans 12:10), "especially of the mutual love of parents and children."[1]

The last, *agape*, is the Greek word that expresses God's love. Biblical scholars believe this obscure Greek term (found only once in all Greek literature) was coined in the New Testament to define God's love.[2] *Agape* love is an unselfish choice for the good of another, the choice to give to, lay down your life for, serve and bless the people around you. It can be pictured as a parent who has one beloved child, for whom the parent pours out all his affections and sacrifices.[3] This use of *agape* was revolutionary, totally different from Old Testament and rabbinical teachings, for Jesus revealed that God loves those who are His enemies; thus we are to love our enemies as well (Romans 5:8–10; Matthew 5:43–48).[4]

Learning to Love

If God is love (1 John 4:8, 16) and we are to be like Him, then we need to love as He has loved us. The way I measure my Christlike maturity and love is by how well I love my wife and children. It begins with the people closest to me and fans out to the rest of my relationships, including the unbelievers I encounter in life.

Christlike character begins with loving the most important person in my life: my wife. For the greater part of our 36-plus years of marriage, it has been amazing; but we hit a wall in 1992. We had a big fight. I joke today that it began with me saying, "How can God make you beautiful and dumb at the same time?" Sue replied, "God made me beautiful so that you would marry me, but He made me dumb so that I would marry you!"

That is an old joke, but the fight we had was no joking matter. I rejected Sue and spoke harsh words over her that left her emotionally broken. We had had fights before—destructive verbal ones, in which I used my anger and my words to put her down, thereby rejecting her and breaking her heart. But this fight was different. For the first time, she emotionally broke down. Even though I apologized, she stayed emotionally detached and broken. She became depressed, and then the depression hit me. We knew we needed help.

Initially we sought out another pastor for counsel, but the help we got was not good. He diagnosed improperly and stated without much discernment, "Sue is just bitter." He thought she was the problem, and that if she simply repented, things would get better. I was smug and she was hurt. The counselor never suggested that I might be the real culprit, which is usually the case. It does begin with the husband. If I had really loved the way Christ had wanted me to love, she would not have been in the condition she was in.

So we went to another counselor. Sue wanted a professional counselor connected to Fuller School of Psychology. Though our trained counselor was brilliant, and this counseling gave us a "safe place" to talk, we never got the breakthrough. For the sake of our four children, we lived a polite and civil life, but our marriage was drifting. Our sex life was dwindling, and physical affections were perfunctory at best. We looked like we were doing well on the outside, but inside we were hurting deeply.

I have often said (and even published) that 1993 was the worst year of my life. It was mainly because our marriage was suffering. Even during this incredibly dark period, we never threatened to separate, nor did we say the *D* word. Sue jokes that divorce was never an option—murder, yes, but divorce, no. After all, we had made a covenant to stay married in "good times and bad times."

The breakthrough came in a dramatic way. That is why I love the grace of God and the power of the Holy Spirit.

The Toronto Airport Vineyard (now called Catch The Fire, Toronto) was experiencing a powerful revival that broke out when a fellow Vineyard pastor, Randy Clark, spoke at the church on January 20, 1994. The few days of meetings that had been planned were prolonged for twelve years, six nights a week, with an estimated four million-plus visitors. I ended up visiting with a group from our church in October 1994, for their annual Catch The Fire Conference. We were so hungry that the first night of the conference, when they gave an invitation to receive prayer up front, we ran to the platform. More than four thousand people were in attendance.

An elderly lady, perhaps someone's grandmother, came up to me and prayed for me. I did not feel much, but a gentle presence came over me, and with the help of a catcher (usher) I went down on the floor and rested. People were laughing and shaking violently all around me. At first, I was envious. I wanted what the others around me were experiencing. But the Holy Spirit was touching me, and I had a vision: I saw my father's face in my mind's eye, and he was looking at me. I wondered why I was seeing his face. Then God spoke to my heart, *You have been bitter toward your father for many years. You have judged him for rejecting you and abusing you. And now you have become just like your father by rejecting and abusing Sue with your harsh words.*

An overwhelming grief and sorrow came over me. That was the first time I really saw how wrongly I had treated Sue, how harsh and unkind I had been through the years of our marriage. I understood for the first time that I was the problem all along. The deception over my thinking was broken, and I began to weep uncontrollably, which soon turned into tears of deep repentance. I repented of bitterness toward my dad and repented deeply for my lack of love toward Sue.

I got up a changed man. My first impulse was to call her (she had stayed in Pasadena). I wanted to share with her what had happened and ask for her forgiveness. But then I realized that I had done that very thing so often that I was going to have to demonstrate the change in my life through my character. Ephesians 5:25 became my blueprint, even my life verse: "Husbands, love your wives, just as Christ also loved the church and gave Himself for her." I decided that by God's grace I was going to love Sue as Christ loved the Church, by laying down my life for her.

Changed as I was, I had enough experience to know that this was still going to be a process. I knew I had a ways to go. Sue and I continued to see our counselor. Then one day, the counselor said, "I don't think you need to see me anymore. I feel that there has been dramatic progress in your marriage and that you are on your way." I thought this had to be of God. We were paying our counselor $75 per session, and she was basically saying, "Save your money!" I knew the time had come to share with Sue what took place.

I took her on a date to Houston's, a nearby restaurant in Pasadena. After dinner, at the right moment, I began to share what had taken place months before in Toronto. As I began to ask her for forgiveness, I broke down, weeping to the point that I could hardly get the words out. (Even now, twenty years later as I am writing this, I am weeping, thanking God for His mercy and for blessing our marriage.) Seeing my tears and brokenness, she knew. She had known something had happened to me in Toronto but wisely waited for me to initiate and share with her at the right moment. I finally got the words out. I deeply repented before her and asked for her forgiveness. Heaven came down that night at Houston's, and a deep healing took place in our marriage.

We still have our moments of what I call "intense fellowship," like most couples, but I can say with total honesty before God that it has been the best twenty years of our marriage (and one of the main reasons for this book). God wants to bless your marriage and all of your relationships, but *it begins with love and Christlike character*.

How to Grow in Christlike Character

Let me give you three recommendations that have helped me immensely over the years.

Be Full of His Spirit

I cannot overemphasize our need to be filled with the Holy Spirit. He was sent by the Father to help us be holy, as He is holy (1 Peter 1:16). We have a tremendous promise of being transformed into the image of Jesus: "But we all, with unveiled face, beholding as in a mirror the glory of the Lord, are being transformed into the same image from glory to glory, just as by the Spirit of the Lord" (2 Corinthians 3:18).

That is why I love the Holy Spirit so much. The encounter I had in Toronto is just the tip of the iceberg of my transformation over the past 41 years. That is why Paul says in Galatians 5:16–18 (NRSV),

> Live by the Spirit, I say, and do not gratify the desires of the flesh. For what the flesh desires is opposed to the Spirit, and what the Spirit desires is opposed to the flesh; for these are opposed to each other, to prevent you from doing what you want. But if you are led by the Spirit, you are not subject to the law.

Let me encourage you to make a covenant to stay in the river of God. The river of God is a metaphor for the Holy Spirit found in Ezekiel 47. The angel of the Lord leads Ezekiel into waters that are ankle deep, knee deep and waist deep, and then "it was a river that I could not cross; for the water was too deep, water in which one must swim, a river that could not be crossed" (Ezekiel 47:5). You are still in control out to waist-deep water. But when the water is too deep and the current too fast and you cannot cross over, you have lost control.

I took my son Gabriel to the famous Kenai River in Alaska for king salmon fishing for his thirtieth birthday. After we had caught our limit of king salmon, Gabe and I decided to go out with wading boots, which went up to our chests, so we could go sockeye salmon fishing from the shore. We waded into the Kenai River, and when I was just waist deep, the current was so strong and fast that I immediately envisioned myself tripping, the rubber shoes being filled with water and myself carried down the freezing river to my death. I said to Gabe, trying to hide my fears, "Gabe, I don't feel 'led' to go shore fishing. You fish. I'll just watch you from the shore." And I waded back onto the shore for safety.

Wading out and back, I was never out of control, but God wants you to *surrender control of your life to the Holy Spirit*. He is the One who transforms us and manifests the fruit of His Spirit, which is "love, joy, peace, patience, kindness, goodness, faithfulness, gentleness, self-control; against such things there is no law" (Galatians 5:22–23 ESV). To have these, get filled with and stay full of His Spirit.

Cultivate Intimacy with God

Having intimacy with God is another way to grow in Christlike character.

> Abide in Me, and I in you. As the branch cannot bear fruit of itself, unless it abides in the vine, neither can you, unless you abide in Me. I am the vine, you are the branches. He who abides in Me, and I in him, bears much fruit; for without Me you can do nothing.
>
> John 15:4–5

Jesus was referring to fruitfulness in life, but that definitely includes the fruits of the Spirit, and thus Christlike character. For me, intimacy involves spending time with God, meditating on God's Word and spending time in prayer and worship. There are no shortcuts to intimacy. In more than 41 years of walking with the Lord, hardly a day has gone by that I did not spend some time in the Word of God and in prayer.

The psalmist asks, "How can a young person stay pure? By obeying your word. . . . I have hidden your word in my heart, that I might not sin against you" (Psalm 119:9, 11 NLT). Over the years, I have meditated on the Bible to the point that when I preach, Scriptures just flow out of me. A famous commercial asks, "What's in your wallet?" I want to ask, "What's in your heart?"

Make a Commitment to a Local Church

The early Church devoted itself to the apostles' teaching, breaking bread (communion), fellowshiping together and praying together (Acts 2:42). They met in the Temple daily and from house to house, eating together and fellowshiping with one another (Acts 2:46). The early Church was a family. It seems that the early believers were more committed than most families—and most churches—today.

Unfortunately, many Christians presently are not committed to a local church. They might visit on Easter and at

Christmastime. Many are disillusioned; others have been hurt by the Church and want nothing to do with Christians. I know the Church is not perfect—someone said, "If you find the perfect church, once you get there, it won't be perfect because you are there." The Church is God's people called to change the world. Because His people are imperfect, the Church will always be in the process of becoming more like Him. It is, as someone said, "imperfect people trying to live out a new life in a new way."

Even with all of the Church's flaws, I would not be where I am today if I had not been in a local church when I gave my life to Jesus. I received weekly teachings that transformed my life. I was privileged to be mentored and discipled by my senior pastor. I still remember his words of wisdom: "Ché, don't try to be successful. Be faithful, and God will make you a success." I think he got that quote from Mother Teresa, but regardless of the source, to this day I am in pursuit of being faithful and becoming Christlike. I have been extremely blessed through the local church. The Church is vital to your personal growth and accountability. You will also receive a sense of family and community, a critical need on this orphan planet. Most importantly, you will be blessed as you are apostolically aligned.

The blessing of God flows into your life by you being apostolically aligned. Let me explain what I mean as we look at Psalm 133:

Behold, how good and how pleasant it is for brethren to dwell together in unity! It is like the precious oil upon the head, running down on the beard, the beard of Aaron, running down on the edge of his garments. It is like the dew of Hermon, descending upon the mountains of Zion; for there the LORD commanded the blessing—life forevermore.

This psalm was a priestly prayer to affirm one's alignment and covenant commitment with the high priest. Aaron is named in this postexilic psalm because he was the first high priest, which represents the apostolic in the Old Testament. In Hebrews 3:1, the Bible calls Jesus "the Apostle and High Priest of our confession." When we get apostolically aligned and posture our hearts to be in covenant unity with our apostles or pastors, we receive "the commanded blessing" from God Himself.

Let me encourage you to look for an apostolic center, a local church led by a pastor with an apostolic calling. Or look for a church in which your senior pastor is apostolically aligned. I believe if you find a local church that is aligned apostolically and where the Holy Spirit is welcomed and the Bible is preached, you will be blessed big time!

Now declare this decree of blessing over your life:

I decree a blessing over my life that I will be transformed from glory to glory into the image and character of Christ, growing and demonstrating the fruit of the Holy Spirit.

13

Decree #6: God's Kingdom

I decree a blessing over you that you will seek first His Kingdom and His righteousness and will preach the Gospel of the Kingdom with signs and wonders following.

A Kingdom That Stands Forever

Once there was a mighty king in Babylon. Though he was the most powerful king in the world, he was greatly disturbed one night by a dream that he did not understand. So he ordered all of his wise men to give him the interpretation, without having heard the dream—but they could not fulfill his request.

Consequently, the king was so furious he ordered that all of them and their family members be destroyed. When one of the wise men learned of his fate, he prayed to the God of Abraham, Isaac and Jacob. God heard his cry and gave him the dream and its interpretation in an open vision.

This wise man came boldly before the king. "Oh king, live forever. No man can do what you have asked, but there is a God who knows all things. He has revealed this dream to me and has given me the interpretation." He went on to describe a statue the king had seen, composed of different materials, and a rock that struck and destroyed the statue and then grew to become an enormous mountain covering the earth.

The wise man interpreted the parts of the statue to be different empires: The gold head represented the Babylonian Empire; the silver chest an inferior empire to come (which became the empire of the Persians/Medes); the bronze abdomen and thighs a third empire (the Greeks); and, finally, the iron legs a strong empire that would crush the others (the Roman Empire). But the rock the king had seen would be sent by God to shatter the last kingdom, and it would grow until it covered the earth. "That kingdom is the Kingdom of God," the wise man explained, "and its King will rule from that point on!"

The story above is a Ché Ahn paraphrase of Daniel 2—one of the most stunning and important passages in the Bible.

God has a lot to say about His Kingdom. In the four gospels alone, the word *kingdom* (*basileia*) appears 120 times; for comparison, the word *church* (*ekklesia*) shows up only in two verses (Matthew 16:18; 18:17). The Church is not the Kingdom. The Church is to advance God's Kingdom, but they are not the same. The Kingdom is the rule and reign of God and the realm of His presence—in short, heaven on earth (Matthew 6:10).

We learn several truths about God's Kingdom in Daniel 2:

1. Jesus is the King of kings and Lord of lords (Daniel 2:47; Revelation 19:16).
2. His Kingdom rules over all (Daniel 2:35; Psalm 103:19).
3. His Kingdom is eternal (Daniel 2:44; Psalm 145:13; Isaiah 9:7).
4. His Kingdom is advancing: "And the stone that struck the image *became* a great mountain and *filled* the whole earth" (Daniel 2:35, emphasis mine; Matthew 28:18–20).
5. His Kingdom comes in power (Daniel 2:44; 1 Corinthians 4:20).
6. The kingdoms of this world will become the Kingdom of our Lord, and He will reign forever (Daniel 2:44; Revelation 11:15). Note that it only took until the fourth century for the Roman emperor to declare the whole empire Christian.
7. This Kingdom would manifest during the Roman Empire (Daniel 2:43–44).

This Kingdom was prophesied to King David, to whom Nathan the prophet declared this word of the Lord:

When your days are fulfilled and you rest with your fathers, I will set up your seed after you, who will come from your body, and I will establish his kingdom. He shall build a house for My name, and I will establish the throne of his kingdom forever.

2 Samuel 7:12–13

Speaking of clear prophetic words about the coming eternal Messiah, the famous "Christmas" prophecy comes to mind:

For to us a child is born, to us a son is given, and the government will be on his shoulders. And he will be called Wonderful Counselor, Mighty God, Everlasting Father, Prince of *Peace*. Of the greatness of his government and *peace* there will be no end. He will reign on David's throne and over his kingdom, establishing and upholding it with justice and righteousness from that time on and forever.

Isaiah 9:6–7 NIV, emphasis mine

In the fullness of time, these prophecies were fulfilled in Jesus (Galatians 4:4), who came to establish His Kingdom. He recaptured what was lost in the Garden of Eden through His death, resurrection and ascension. Now He is seated at the right hand of the Father, ruling and reigning over the earth (see Ephesians 1:17–23). Since Jesus' appearance two millennia ago, the Kingdom of God has been advancing—and it is still advancing!

What is more, God's will is to advance His Kingdom through *you*. Our magnificent God has called us to co-labor with Him in the most adventurous, exciting purpose in life: to fulfill the Great Commission.

> And Jesus came and spoke to them, saying, "All authority has been given to Me in heaven and on earth. Go therefore and make disciples of all the nations, baptizing them in the name of the Father and of the Son and of the Holy Spirit, teaching them to observe all things that I have commanded you; and lo, I am with you always, even to the end of the age."
>
> Matthew 28:18–20

Born Again to Rule

You were not saved just to go to heaven. You were saved to bring heaven to earth. When Jesus says, "All authority is given to Me in heaven and on earth," He is implying that He has delegated His authority to us. "Behold, I give you the authority to trample on serpents and scorpions, and over all the power of the enemy, and nothing shall by any means hurt you" (Luke 10:19). The authority the King of kings gives is for advancing His Kingdom. You take it up as kings and priests (Revelation 1:6; 5:10; 1 Peter 2:9), who are seated with Him in heavenly places in a position of rule and authority (Ephesians 1:20; 2:6).

Only twice in my life has my spirit left my body and gone into heaven; the second time, God showed me what it means to be sitting with Him in heavenly places. On a Sunday in 2004, people were praying for me before our service in Mott Auditorium. Weighing on my mind was a looming deadline to raise $3.5 million. The door had opened for HRock Church to purchase the famous Ambassador Auditorium in Pasadena. Called the "Carnegie Hall of the West" for its outstanding acoustics, it has been compared to the Dorothy Chandler Pavilion for its beauty and has hosted artists such as Luciano Pavarotti, Arthur Rubinstein, Pearl Bailey, Yo-Yo Ma and the Vienna Boys' Choir.

The building was valued at more than $20 million, but it was offered to us for $12 million, so long as we could raise $4.5 million in cash for the down payment—in four months. We had put $1 million down immediately as a security deposit, which we would lose if we could not come up with the balance. I have to admit I was envisioning headlines on the front page of the *Los Angeles Times*: "Pastor of HRock Church Loses $1 Million of the Church's Money in Real Estate Deal."

On that Sunday morning, the deadline for the down payment was two months away. As the people were praying for me, I began to manifest the Spirit of God, jumping up and down as if I were on a pogo stick. It was embarrassing, but I knew that God was doing this through my yielded body.

All of a sudden, as I jumped, my spirit left my body and went into heaven. I could see the silhouette of Jesus on His throne with the glory cloud all around Him. I immediately went into His body, and I heard the Lord say, *You are seated with me in the heavenly places.* As soon as I heard this, I was back in my body at Mott Auditorium.

When I returned to my body, I knew Ambassador Auditorium was a done deal. With four days to go, we still had to raise $1.3 million. When the pastors asked me how we were we going to get $1.3 million in four days, I declared what I had been decreeing since this heavenly encounter: "It's a done deal."

In the end, God parted the Red Sea in front of us. The money came through the generosity of one dear friend, who, with his wife, gave us $1.3 million. By 4:00 p.m. on the day it was due, we had the $4.5 million, which we quickly wired to consummate the purchase of this magnificent property. HRock Church became the owner of one of the premier performance arts buildings in the world.

We have used the auditorium for many events to serve our city, before which the Gospel is always presented in a concise and tasteful way. When the Pasadena mayor, Bill Bogaard, came to honor our church on the tenth anniversary of our ownership, he announced that, according to his calculations, we had reached more than 120,000 people with the Gospel who would not normally have come to our services!

How Are We to Advance the Kingdom?

You have this same authority to loose resources to advance His Kingdom. Here are ways to exercise it:

1. First, make Jesus the King and Lord of your life. Matthew 6:33 states, "But seek first the kingdom of God and His righteousness, and all these things shall be added to you." If you have not made Jesus the Lord of your life, let me repeat the prayer that I wrote for you in chapter 5: *Jesus, forgive me for my sins. I give You my heart, my whole life. I make You the Lord of my life. By Your grace, I will follow You and obey You all the days of my life. In Jesus' name, amen.*

2. Advance God's Kingdom by praying, "Thy kingdom come, Thy will be done!" (Matthew 6:10 KJV). The verbs in this verse are in the imperative tense—God wants us to command Him to bring heaven to earth! That is how the Kingdom advances. There is no sickness in heaven, so we say, "On earth as it is in heaven." There is no poverty, so we say, "On earth as it is in heaven." There is no injustice, no racism, no one demonized—the list goes on. God is after not only salvation for humanity but also social transformation. Incidentally, you will never find the phrase *the Gospel of salvation* in the Bible. You find only *the Gospel of the Kingdom.*

3. Advance His Kingdom by preaching the Gospel of the Kingdom with signs and wonders following (Matthew 24:14; Mark 16:15–18). I will share about moving in signs and wonders in the next decree.

Finally, let me encourage you to be Kingdom minded and Kingdom hearted. My mentor, Dr. Peter Wagner, teaches this with the picture of a three-rung Kingdom Ladder. The first rung, on which most stand, is a focus on self. People focus on healing and blessing for themselves, which is not wrong in itself; but if that is all you focus on, you become self-absorbed and ultimately unfulfilled. Remember that the blessing is for a purpose. The second rung on the ladder is a focus on the Church. People on this rung want their churches to grow and be blessed. That is good, but we should not stop there. The third rung is our ultimate focus, a focus on the Kingdom. When you seek first the Kingdom of God, advancing His Kingdom by being a blessing to others, God will take care of your needs and those of your church.

This became a living parable for me from 2000 to 2003, when the Lord spoke to me clearly to lay down my ministry as pastor of HRock Church and leader of HIM. He told me to put everything on pause and delegate my responsibilities away so I could help Lou Engle with his vision for TheCall, an assembling of young people to pray and fast for revival in our nation. Lou was a good friend and my associate pastor at the time. We ended up mobilizing more than 400,000 young people on September 2, 2000, for the first TheCall event. We held six more events during the next three years, the smallest of which drew 30,000 people on a very cold November day at the Cotton Bowl Stadium in Dallas, Texas.

In three years of serving Lou and TheCall, during which I, the senior pastor, was gone three out of four Sundays every month, our church went through a Gideon's revival—attendance dropped from 1,100 to 550 people! It was hard, but I had no regrets. I knew I was obeying God by advancing His Kingdom through TheCall. And since my resignation as president of TheCall, our attendance has more than tripled and God gave us the Ambassador Auditorium. Hallelujah! Be Kingdom minded and Kingdom hearted, because His blessings will overflow exceedingly beyond what you can think or ask (Ephesians 3:20).

Now declare this decree over your life:

> *I decree a blessing over my life that I will seek first His Kingdom and His righteousness, and I will preach the Gospel of the Kingdom with signs and wonders following.*

14

Decree #7: Healing and Blessing

I decree a blessing over you that God will heal you physically, that you will walk in divine health and that God will use you to heal others.

A Kingdom Paradigm Shift

One of the most exciting signs that we are in a global revival is that amazing miracles and healings are taking place all around the world. These healings are not confined to the developing continents of Africa, Latin America and parts of Asia; they are occurring in the Western world and even in the good old U.S. of A.

In April 2013, I was with dear friends and spiritual children Steven and Rene Springer at their apostolic center in

Madison, Wisconsin. I had just finished speaking at a Friday night healing service and was on my way back to the auditorium for a book signing. A young lady jumped out of her seat and grabbed me to ask if I would pray for her right eye. "I was born blind in my right eye," she said. "I am totally blind in it."

I remembered the story of how Jesus spit in the eye of a blind man. Not to worry—I did not spit in her eye, but I did something that I felt the Lord was leading me to do. I licked my right thumb with my saliva and placed it on her right eye and made a decree, commanding the eye to be opened. When I took my hand off, she started to scream. She said, "Oh my God! I can't believe my eye is open! I can see!"

To be totally honest, I could not believe it either! I have seen several blind people get healed in more than forty years of praying for the sick, but it always shocks me when a blind eye is opened. Even more amazing is that she had suffered from scoliosis all her life, on top of which her back and neck had been injured in a recent car accident. When I placed my thumb on her eye, she said later, "I felt power go through my eye, through my neck and throughout my back. I felt as if I were being adjusted by a chiropractor. All my pain in my back and neck are gone!"[1] God does exceedingly and abundantly more than we can ask or think (Ephesians 3:20).

Jesus began His ministry by preaching, "Repent, for the kingdom of heaven is at hand" (Matthew 4:17). Though the word *repent* does carry the meaning of turning from your sins, literally it "signifies to change one's mind or purpose."[2] The meaning comes from the Greek word *metanoeo*, composed of *meta* ("after") and *nous* ("mind" or "perception")—hence a change of mind. Today we would call it a paradigm shift. Let me give you my paraphrase of the verse: "Many of you believed that after death you will go to heaven, but I want you to have a paradigm shift and believe that you can experience heaven now."

The Lord's Prayer that we have been praying for two thousand years supports this truth: "Our Father in heaven, hallowed be Your name. Your kingdom come. Your will be done on earth as it is in heaven" (Matthew 6:9–10). On earth as it is in heaven. Why is it important that we receive healing from God? Because in heaven there is no sickness. In heaven no one runs around demonized with addictions or depression. That is God's will for you on earth as well. Which is why, after telling His followers that the Kingdom of heaven is at hand, Jesus goes out to heal the sick and cast out demons.

And Jesus went about all Galilee, teaching in their synagogues, preaching the gospel of the kingdom, and healing all kinds of sickness and all kinds of disease among the people. Then His fame went throughout all Syria; and they brought to Him all sick people who were afflicted with various diseases and torments, and those who were demon-possessed, epileptics, and paralytics; and He healed them.

Matthew 4:23–24

Notice that He healed *all* the sick people who came to Him. This is no generalization. In heaven you do not see 99 percent healed and 1 percent sick. All are healed and healthy in heaven (whatever that looks like with our heavenly bodies).

God Wants to Heal You

Is it God's will that everyone be healed? I say a definitive yes! Even without supernatural manifestations of healing, we experience healing all the time. The psalmist says, "I will praise You, for I am fearfully and wonderfully made" (Psalm 139:14). God has built a healing mechanism into your body, called the immune system, which attacks every invading virus or organism to kill it and make you well again. Recently, I had a paper cut on my finger. I said, "Jesus, heal me" (paper cuts are, for whatever reason, the most painful). That evening as I was typing on my computer, I realized that my finger was healed. Did God heal me? Yes and no. I was not healed immediately; the pain and the cut bothered me throughout the day. By that evening, though, my finger was healed because my body healed itself. Your body is healing itself all the time, every second sending minerals and organic materials to the parts that need healing. That is the way God beautifully and fearfully designed us—He is the One who ultimately heals.

God also heals us through doctors and medicine. I respect the medical community and am actually surrounded by physicians: My brother, my brother-in-law and my parents-in-law are all physicians. Thanks to advances in medical fields, we are much healthier now than in years past. Steven More writes, "The health of Americans improved in ways during the 20th Century that can only be described as miraculous."[3] He goes on to say, "Before 1900 major killers included such infectious diseases as tuberculosis, smallpox, diphtheria, polio, influenza, and bronchitis. Just three infectious diseases—tuberculosis, pneumonia, and diarrhea—accounted for almost half of all deaths in 1900. Now few Americans die from these diseases, and many diseases have been completely eradicated due to a medley of modern medicines."[4]

Finally, if you do not believe that God wants to heal all people totally, remember that we are ultimately healed when we die and go to heaven. Every believer will receive a new heavenly body, and no matter what sicknesses were not healed supernaturally, naturally or by doctors and medicine, God guarantees us total healing in the life to come.

My mother went home to be with the Lord after fighting liver cancer for a number of years. In the late '90s, she had minor surgery, and during a blood transfusion, the blood she received was tainted with hepatitis C. She contracted hepatitis C, which advanced into cirrhosis of the liver and then cancer of the liver. (I did not say the medical community is perfect, but I still thank God for them.) She reacted violently to chemotherapy and chose not to receive further treatment. Amazingly, she lived three years longer than the doctors had projected. The whole time, my mother and our family believed for a supernatural healing. I have seen too many cancers healed supernaturally by God for me not to believe. I was at her bedside a few days before she slipped into a coma, and then on May 3, 2002, she went home to be with the Lord. I was tremendously sad and disappointed. I also felt terrible that I was not by her bedside, having traveled and ministered to God's people while she was dying in the hospital.

Around a month after my mom passed away, I had an extraordinary encounter with the Lord. I was lying on the floor of Mott Auditorium, spending time with the Lord and soaking up His presence, when all of a sudden I was out of my body! I could see my body lying on the floor of the auditorium, and my spirit went into heaven, where I met my mother. I had read about Paul visiting heaven in 2 Corinthians 12:1–4, and I had heard of other people's experiences (I think of the book *Heaven Is for Real*), but I had never gone up to heaven before. Nor was my mother on my radar. This had to be the Lord.

My mother passed away when she was seventy, but in heaven she looked like she was in her twenties (I am sure some of you cannot wait to get there!). She told me there were many things she had wanted to communicate to me before she passed away, and now Jesus was giving her an opportunity to tell me. All the instructions pertained to my dad. She told me to invite Dad to Korea to speak at an HIM conference. I was to fly my dad over in business class and give him a generous honorarium. I was to take my dad on a golfing vacation and spend quality time with him. She instructed me how to love my dad in his own love language. After she spoke to me, my spirit was back in my body and I lay weeping on the floor.

What encouraged me more than anything was the reality that my mother was totally healed of cancer and had a beautiful new body. I knew it to be true theologically, but to see it—to encounter it—the truth became revelatory.

God wants to heal all people. Some will be healed naturally and through our amazing immune systems. Some will be healed through doctors. All of us will be healed when death and sickness are totally conquered, either when we go home to be with Jesus or when Jesus returns to us on the earth. But what I am contending for you in this decree is God's supernatural healing.

Before we talk about God's healing power, I want to talk about the higher way: walking in divine health. This is God's will, for the Bible says in 3 John 2, "Beloved, I pray that you may prosper in all things and *be in health*, just as your soul prospers" (emphasis mine). Receiving God's healing is wonderful, but walking in divine health is significantly superior and God's will for your life.

Divine health combines the supernatural power of God to keep us in health with a personal commitment to living a healthy lifestyle. We live in the supernatural as we do our part by simply eating nutritious meals and exercising on a regular basis. I have not always done this, and I was constantly sick. Then I began eating properly—no sugar or bad carbs and plenty of vegetables, fruits and good protein—and exercising, and I have walked in divine health for more than fifteen years.

Blessing Others by Healing the Sick

One of the greatest joys I have as a leader in the Church is seeing God raise up an army of His children to heal the sick and move in signs and wonders. When he was my professor at Fuller, John Wimber used to say, "He is equipping the saints to do the stuff," meaning heal the sick, cast out demons and raise the dead (see Mark 16:17–18). That means you.

This year I heard one of the most amazing healing testimonies I have ever heard at Voice of the Apostles, an annual conference hosted by Randy Clark. A woman shared that, during the birth of her son (who is now fifteen years old), she suffered severe nerve damage to her pelvic region, leaving her bedridden and in pain for years. She had seven surgeries before finally flying to France to see a specialist. While in surgery there, she hemorrhaged to death; her spirit left her body, and she was floating in the operating room.

Free from the pain, she heard the Lord say she could choose to go to heaven now or return to her body. He let her see her son, who was still a little boy. She knew that if she died and went to heaven, her son would be hurt and bitter toward God and potentially never give his heart to Him. She knew she had to go back to her family. As soon as she was in her body again, she felt excruciating pain. After thirteen more surgeries in fourteen years, she recovered a little, but the only time she was without pain was when she was on her back or on her knees.

This woman came to the Voice of the Apostles conference in 2012. During ministry time, an elderly man approached her and asked, "Can I pray for you?" He was on his way to the men's room, and he heard the Lord say, *Go pray for that woman*. He prayed, but she was not healed.

He came back later, asking, "How are you doing?"

"I am the same," she answered, "but that is all right."

"No, that is not all right," he replied. "God healed me, He healed my wife and He healed my son—and He is going to heal *you*!" He began to minister deliverance to her, commanding spirits of death, sickness and suicide and other demons to come out of her. The woman felt the demons leaving. Then he placed one finger over her stomach and commanded the pain to leave her in Jesus' name. For the first time in years, she felt no pain. He asked her to do something that she had previously been unable to do. She was on her knees, and she had not been able to stand up without excruciating pain. When she stood to her feet, she knew she was totally healed—and she has been healed since.[5]

Who was the man who prayed for this lady? I do not know. But that nameless and faceless man represents people like you. God wants to use you to be a blessing to others by healing the sick, casting out demons and even raising the dead.

This is Jesus' commission to you:

> Go into all the world and preach the gospel to every creature. . . . And these signs will follow those who *believe*: In My name they will cast out demons; they will speak with new tongues; they will take up serpents; and if they drink anything deadly, it will by no means hurt them; they will lay hands on the sick, and they will recover.
>
> Mark 16:15, 17–18, emphasis mine

If you are a believer, the Bible says you can do all these things. Just believe!

Now decree this blessing over your life, out loud and by faith:

> *I decree a blessing over me that God will heal me physically, that I will walk in divine health and that God will use me to heal others.*

15

Decree #8: Family

I decree a blessing over all your relationships, beginning with your family: that God would bless your marriage and the fruit of your womb; that He would bless your children, your grandchildren and your friendships in His Church and in the marketplace; and that your entire family would be saved.

Blessing the Fruit of Your Womb

As I was trying to meet the January deadline for this book, my daughter Joy texted me to ask if Sue and I could come over to her home for dinner. Joy and her husband, Kuoching, wanted to give us our Christmas gift early (it was December 18). Sue and I were immediately curious. We asked each other as we drove to their house, "What kind of gift is so time sensitive that they want to give it to us early and privately?"

We had a wonderful dinner and enjoyed playing with my two-year-old granddaughter, Annabelle. After dinner, Joy brought out the gift. In a simple, green gift bag was a picture frame. *Huh?* I thought. *That's not exactly a time-sensitive gift.* The frame had a beautiful picture of Annabelle. She was wearing a sweatshirt with these words across her chest: "I am going to be a big sister." It took us a few seconds for the words to register, and then Sue and I began to weep for joy. This was Joy and Kuoching's creative way to honor us with the news that they were expecting their second child.

One of the major signs that God is blessing you is your fruitfulness in life. That is how I interpret John 15:8, in which Jesus said, "By this my Father is glorified, that you bear much fruit and so prove to be my disciples" (ESV). God is for you and not against you—He wants you to bear fruit. I think Jesus was covering everything from the fruit of the Spirit (Galatians 5:22–23) to being productive in life. The Bible specifically declares, however, that God wants to bless the fruit of your womb:

> He will love you and bless you and multiply you; He will also bless the fruit of your womb and the fruit of your land, your grain and your new wine and your oil, the increase of your cattle and the offspring of your flock, in the land of which He swore to your fathers to give you. You shall be blessed

above all peoples; there shall not be a male or female barren among you or among your livestock.

Deuteronomy 7:13–14

Twice this important passage states that God specifically wants to bless the fruit of your womb. ("There shall not be a male or female barren among you.") This is underscored further when God enumerates the blessings that will overcome His covenant people. The famous blessing chapter in the Bible, Deuteronomy 28, includes this promise:

> And all these blessings shall come upon you and overtake you, because you obey the voice of the LORD your God: . . . Blessed shall be the fruit of your body, the produce of your ground and the increase of your herds, the increase of your cattle and the offspring of your flocks.

Deuteronomy 28:2, 4

God wants you blessed, and a major way for you to be blessed is to be fruitful and multiply—literally. From the very beginning, God blessed Adam and Eve for a purpose: "Be fruitful and multiply; fill the earth and subdue it; have dominion over the fish of the sea, over the birds of the air, and over every living thing that moves on the earth" (Genesis 1:28). This was God's mandate to man and woman before the Fall. His purpose has not changed. He still wants us to be fruitful, to multiply, to subdue the enemy and to rule and reign with Him over the earth. Specifically, He wants to bless you with as many children as you want.

Why is this? One thought is that God is love and He wants a big family to love. That is why He has given us the Great Commission. The mandate in Genesis 1:28 still stands. God anticipates that a spiritual legacy will be passed down from generation to generation. He has confidence that your children and your grandchildren will know Him and walk with Him all the days of their lives.

Secondly, He wants His Kingdom to advance. The Bible says, "The kingdom of God is within you" (Luke 17:21). As we discussed in the previous decrees, when God's people multiply, they bring the Kingdom of God wherever they go. They shift the atmosphere by bringing heaven to earth. As they multiply, His Kingdom naturally advances.

The Roman Catholic Church is a good example of this. It became the largest branch of Christianity in the world without aggressively evangelizing like evangelical denominations. Catholics influence public policy in nations where their numbers are strong (such as keeping abortion illegal in Ireland, the Philippines and Latin America). Catholics have grown in number because they have a beautiful culture of life, valuing it in all forms. It is not unusual for devout Catholics to have large families.

Another religious group that has grown through biological means is Islam. Muslim families in the United States average 2.8 children per couple, whereas the rest of American families average 2.1 children per couple.[1] It may not seem like a big difference, but eventually, this level of biological growth combined with an influx of Muslim immigrants will allow Muslims to impact public policy in the United States. This is already happening in Europe.

I am not saying this to be alarmist, only as an example. I have a positive eschatology: "The kingdoms of this world have become the kingdoms of our Lord and of His Christ, and He shall reign forever and ever!" (Revelation 11:15). Just imagine if Spirit-filled, Kingdom-minded Christians started having large families. Think of the enormous blessing they could bring to the world. You and I are the salt of the earth and the light of the world. You were created to be a blessing to others. More of God's people who demonstrate His blessing and His love in tangible ways will bring nations to Jesus Christ.

For those who have lost a baby due to miscarriage or still-birth, my heart goes out to you. I have close family members who have lost their babies, including my daughter, my sister and my mother, who miscarried a son that would have been my older brother. The Holy Spirit is the Comforter. Let Him comfort you and your family. With all my heart I believe that all babies go to heaven, and that you will be reunited with your child (see 2 Samuel 12:22–23). For now, let the God who came to heal the brokenhearted (Luke 4:18) heal you of that loss.

For those who are contending for a baby, I decree that God will bless the fruit of your womb and you will get pregnant!

I feel I have an anointing to pray for this. Let me share one testimony that appears in my book *How To Pray for Healing*: I was approached by a woman who asked me to pray that she could have a baby. Though she and her husband had been married for seven years, she could not conceive, despite spending thousands of dollars on treatments. Her husband was ready to leave her because she could not give him a child.

As I prayed for her, the Lord spoke to me, and to my astonishment I prophesied that she would have a child within the year! As soon as I said it, I wanted to take it back, because putting a time limit on a prophecy is a risky business. But it was too late—she had already fallen to the floor under the power of the Holy Spirit. I had to trust God on the matter. A month after that, she approached me, beaming, to say she was already three weeks pregnant. She and her husband gave their lives to the Lord then, and we dedicated their beautiful baby girl in our church nine months later.[2]

Here is another testimony: Nelson and Jenny were sent by the Chinese government to Pasadena so Nelson could get his doctorate at the California Institute of Technology. They became Christians while in the U.S. They wanted to have a baby, but Jenny had had constant menstruation for more than ten years and had found no medical solution. They came to me after one Sunday morning service at HRock and asked for prayer to be healed of the bleeding and, more importantly, to conceive and have a baby. As I was praying for them, I had a prophetic word that they would have two children. Six months later, they approached me to share the good news that Jenny was healed and pregnant. Back in China, she gave birth to a boy, whose picture they sent me.

Two years later, I was speaking in Hong Kong. To my surprise (because they live in Shanghai), Jenny and Nelson were in the audience. They had flown to Hong Kong to meet me and show me that Jenny was six months pregnant with their second child! I give glory to God, because the prophetic word came to pass and because she was able to conceive both children while she was in her early forties.

Blessing Your Family with Quality Time

People have asked Sue and me for the secret to raising children who know God at a young age, walk with Him throughout their adult years and are successful in life. If there is one thing that has been the key to our success, it is spending quality time as a family.

I remember hearing James Dobson say on the radio, "Children spell *love* T-I-M-E." I have found it to be very true. When we were new parents, Sue had to mentor me in this area. Her love language is time, so naturally her love was expressed to our children and to me by spending quality time with us.

I grew up never spending quality time with my parents. They never took a day off. My parents were busy with ministry and my dad's dental lab (his "tent making" job was as a dental technician). I cannot remember my family ever taking a family vacation; they were just trying to survive financially as immigrants in this great country. So quality time was not of high value in our home. But Sue's parents valued time. Though her mom was a very successful pediatrician, she temporarily gave up her practice to raise her children. I am grateful for that heritage.

When we got married, Sue and I consistently had a weekly date. Now, after 35 years of marriage, we still "date" every Monday, our day off, whenever I am not on the road. It is also our goal to pray together every day for our children, grandchildren and the specific needs of our family and our church. Even when I am traveling, we try to connect daily for updates and prayer. Thank God for FaceTime! Because this is a strong value in our lives, by God's grace, we have been fairly consistent in praying together.

When we started having children, we had "family day" once a week. Now we have family *night*, sort of like holding Thanksgiving dinner every week. We are grateful that all of our children and grandchildren live in the vicinity of Pasadena (did I mention that we are blessed?). Every Monday night, the kids bring the grandchildren and a contribution to the meal (we usually provide the main course), and we have a weekly family dinner. This may not be your norm, but spending quality time in the context of your situation should be your objective.

God's Blessing and Family Salvation

I believe that God has saved you to save your family. In the New Testament, we see households getting saved en masse. For example, Cornelius "had called together his relatives and close friends" (Acts 10:24) when Peter was summoned to his home. Everyone came to know Jesus when Peter preached the Gospel, and they were all filled with the Holy Spirit (Acts 10:44–47). Later in the Book of Acts, the Philippian jailer and his household came to Christ. Paul makes a statement that I want every reader to decree and claim for their unbelieving family members: "Believe on the Lord Jesus Christ, and you will be saved, you and your household" (Acts 16:31). Sue and I have decreed this over our family and relatives, and we can testify, by the grace of God, that we have seen our entire generation of family members and relatives come to know Christ.[3]

Now decree this blessing over your life and over your family in faith:

> *I decree a blessing over all my relationships, beginning with my family: that God would bless my marriage and the fruit of my womb; that God would bless my children, my grandchildren and my friendships in His Church and in the marketplace; and that my entire family would be saved.*

16

Decree #9: Prosperity

*I decree a blessing over your finances, that God will
break the spirit of poverty off you and your bloodline
and that you will prosper financially; that God would
bless you with the power to gain wealth; and that you
would advance His Kingdom with your generosity.*

Breaking the Spirit of Poverty

At the end of the evening at a conference, two men in their
forties, dressed casually in blue jeans, wanted to have a few
words with me. One of them said, "We are Catholic priests."
They were not wearing the traditional collar, and they noticed
that I was looking at their clothing. "We don't always dress
like priests. We wanted to comment on what you said as you
received the offering tonight."

My heart froze. I had spoken about how the spirit of poverty had come into the Catholic Church around the fourth century through the influence of the heresy of Gnosticism. Gnostics believed that the material world (that is, all matter) is evil and that only the spiritual world is good. When the monastic movement emerged shortly after, members of the various orders made vows of chastity, poverty and obedience. From that period on, a mental shift took place in which poverty was equated with piety, and, I believe, a spirit of poverty entered the Church. During the offering, I made a decree to break the spirit of poverty over the people at the conference. I was certain I had offended the priests, and that they wanted to rebuke me.

The priest continued. "We agree with what you said. On behalf of the Catholic Church, will you forgive us for bringing the spirit of poverty into the Body of Christ?" (This is called identification repentance. You can find examples of it in Daniel 9, Nehemiah 9 and Ezra 9.)

What a shock. I was bracing myself for correction, but these godly priests humbled themselves instead, admitting the Catholic Church's role in releasing a spirit of poverty into the Church and asking forgiveness.

God wants to break the spirit of poverty off of you and your bloodline. If God wants you to prosper, then it stands to reason that Satan wants you poor; the thief comes to steal, kill and destroy (John 10:10). Everywhere I have traveled around the world, I have seen the spirit of poverty over God's children. It may be the reason why you have not received your financial breakthrough. Through this decree, however, I believe that it will be broken off your life and your family.

God Wants to Bless You Financially

Not only do we need to break off the spirit of poverty, we need to receive a revelation that God *does* want us to prosper financially. Here is what the Word of God says about prosperity:

- "The LORD will grant you abundant prosperity . . . in the land he swore to your ancestors to give you" (Deuteronomy 28:11 NIV).

- "Beloved, I pray that in all respects you may prosper and be in good health, just as your soul prospers" (3 John 2 NASB).

- "But remember the LORD your God, for it is he who gives you the ability [power] to produce wealth, and so confirms his covenant, which he swore to your ancestors, as it is today" (Deuteronomy 8:18 NIV).

- "Wealth and honor come from you; you are the ruler of all things. In your hands are strength and power to exalt and give strength to all" (1 Chronicles 29:12 NIV).

- "The blessing of the LORD makes a person rich, and he adds no sorrow with it" (Proverbs 10:22 NLT).

Notice that the Bible specifically states that God wants to bless you with wealth or riches. There is nothing ambiguous about those words—they mean "money." God wants to bless you with financial prosperity. It may be hard to receive this truth; I once had a hard time with it myself, but when I received the revelation that God wants to bless me financially, I started to prosper. "For as he thinks within himself, so he is" (Proverbs 23:7 NASB).

Look at God's promise to Abram: "I will make you a great nation; I will bless you and make your name great; and you shall be a blessing. I will bless those who bless you, and I will curse him who curses you; and in you all the families of the earth shall be blessed" (Genesis 12:2–3). How did God bless Abram? Genesis 13:2 says, "Abram was very rich in livestock, in silver, and in gold." Gold, silver and livestock are valuable commodities even today. God wants you to prosper financially. Jesus says, "So if you sinful people know how to give good gifts to your children, how much more will your heavenly Father give good gifts to those who ask him" (Matthew 7:11 NLT). If I want to bless my children and my grandchildren financially, how much more does our loving heavenly Father want to bless you?

These are not isolated passages. God's blessing throughout the Scriptures is directly or indirectly equated with financial prosperity.

The blessing of Psalm 67, which we discussed in chapter 6, is a financial one: "Then the earth will yield its harvests, and God, our God, will richly bless us. Yes, God will bless us, and people all over the world will fear him" (verses 6–7 NLT). The harvest in this psalm is literally of agricultural produce, and in an agrarian culture, a great harvest means financial prosperity. We are not talking about ordinary prosperity. The psalmist speaks of prosperity and blessing so extraordinary that it will cause nations to fear and reverence God. I do not know what this blessing will look like, but I do know it will be something greater than what we are experiencing now. My guess is that such a tremendous transfer of wealth will come to God's people that the nations—including the Jews—will come to know the Lord (Romans 11:1–26). There is much more prosperity in store for us. The best is yet to come.

Power to Gain Wealth

In *The Great Transfer of Wealth*, Peter Wagner unpacks the meaning of having power to gain wealth (Deuteronomy 8:18). First, God will supernaturally transfer wealth to His people, as He did through the Egyptians, who gave "articles of silver, articles of gold, and clothing" (Exodus 3:21–22) to the departing Israelites in the Exodus.

Secondly, wealth is transferred through wealth creation. "Wealth creators who are kingdom-minded acknowledge that in some manner they have been supernaturally empowered by God in at least three ways," he writes: God "creates [people] with the inherent ability to generate wealth"; He "enhances the recipient's ideas and skills," helping them move forward and improve so that "every year they do better than the year before"; and He imparts new ideas and skills, providing "the creativity to latch onto witty inventions and productive abilities they never had before."[1]

Finally, wealth comes through wealth repossession, the recovery of wealth after it was wrongly taken, either through a stolen inheritance or stolen goods or a rectification of an illegal transaction.

I have to smile at a recent example of wealth repossession in my family. Last year, my Uncle Cho informed me that the government of South Korea had contacted him to reimburse money from land stolen from my grandfather by the government under the late dictator Park Chung-Hee. Years ago, the government rationalized taking land from citizens without proper remuneration by saying that it needed to do whatever it took to develop Korea. My grandfather's land was confiscated to build a highway. Park's daughter, Park Chung-Hae, is the new president of Korea, and somehow her administration contacted my uncle to say the government would reimburse the Cho family with the value of the land in today's real estate market, plus interest.

According to my grandfather's will, his inheritance went to my grandmother, who lived to be 101 before she passed away last August, and his remaining children. Because so many of his children have passed away, including my parents, part of the inheritance was passed to me. That is why I am smiling! You should, too, because God is going to restore what the enemy has stolen from you and your family.

Advance God's Kingdom with Your Generosity

Sue and I made an extraordinary commitment to our Lord in 2005. We had just heard our good friend Ed Silvoso share how financial breakthrough, revival and reformation were taking place among Christian businessmen in Argentina as they formed the 51 Club. Anyone could join this club; members just had to pledge to give over 51 percent of their income to God.

Sue and I were provoked. "Why should the businesspeople have all the fun?" I asked her. "Why don't we give 51 percent?"

"Just 51 percent?" she said. "That's nothing—my goal is that we give away 90 percent and live off the 10 percent!"

I said, "You have more faith than I do. Let's begin by shooting for 51 percent."

We were already giving away 40 percent of our income before taxes, which had been a real stretch. We knew that we could not jump to our goal right away; it had taken us years of gradually increasing our giving to get to 40 percent. But we made the commitment that day to increase giving to 51 percent.

In 2011, my CPA, who was doing my 2010 taxes, called. "Guess what? You gave away over 50 percent of your income last year!" We had reached our goal! Two months later, I received a phone call from a spiritual son who lives in Taiwan. He was on a business trip in New York, and he was stopping in L.A. on his way home. He wanted to buy me lunch, so we made arrangements to meet after our second Sunday morning service.

During lunch, my friend became somber. He said, "Papa Ché, I have talked to my wife, and we have prayed about this. We want to give you a gift, but under certain conditions. You cannot give this gift to the church, or to HIM, or to your church building project. This is just for you and your family."

In the past, when I was under a spirit of poverty, I would have objected, and if a gift were given, I would have turned it over to the church. One sign of a spirit of poverty is the inability to receive. But I have grown since then, so I nodded in agreement with my friend's condition.

"My wife and I want to give you 200,000 shares of our company stock," he said. I was surprised and blessed but immediately curious. How much were they worth? Were they penny stocks? I asked him outright.

He said, "I forgot to tell you! They are worth $2.50 right now, but if you hold on to them, I believe that their value will go up to $9 or $10 a share."

I could not believe what I was hearing. He was giving me $500,000 worth of shares of his company, with the potential of quadrupling it in the future! I could hear the Lord laughing over me. *You think you are sacrificing so much by giving*

Me 51 percent, I heard Him say. *But don't you know that I can out-give you in a heartbeat?*

It is not a cliché that you cannot out-give God. It is truth established on the Word of God.

I am in no way saying that you have to give away 51 percent of your money. Start by tithing—that is a good place to begin. If you are tithing, pray about giving more. Better yet, pray about graduated giving led by His Holy Spirit. We did not start out giving 50 percent. You have to start somewhere and do something. Whatever you do, remember that God loves a cheerful giver, so be led by His Spirit and motivated by grace. As you are generous with what God has given to you, you will prosper:

- "A generous person will prosper; whoever refreshes others will be refreshed" (Proverbs 11:25 NIV).

- "Remember the words of the Lord Jesus, that He said, 'It is more *blessed* to give than to receive'" (Acts 20:35, emphasis mine).

- "But this I say: He who sows sparingly will also reap sparingly, and he who sows bountifully will also reap bountifully" (2 Corinthians 9:6).

The Blessing of Tithing

When you receive the revelation that He has prospered you for a purpose—to advance the Kingdom of God by being a blessing to others—you enter into the law of reciprocity, also known as the law of sowing and reaping. The process is simple: God blesses you to be a blessing to others, and in the process, you reap more blessings so that you can bless others more . . . and so it goes on.

> "Bring the whole tithe into the storehouse, so that there may be food in My house, and test Me now in this," says the LORD of hosts, "if I will not open for you the windows of heaven and pour out for you a blessing until it overflows. Then I will rebuke the devourer for you, so that it will not destroy the fruits of the ground; nor will your vine in the field cast its grapes," says the LORD of hosts. "All the nations will call you blessed, for you shall be a delightful land," says the LORD of hosts.
>
> Malachi 3:10–12 NASB

See how this ties into the theme of God's blessing in the Bible? (1) You bring your tithe (10 percent) to God's storehouse (the church); (2) God opens the windows of heaven and pours out overflowing blessings; (3) you will prosper financially (fruits and vines will flourish); (4) nations will call you blessed. *The blessing of God is the key to world evangelization.* I have heard that if every Christian gave 10 percent of his or her income, then the Church could easily eradicate systemic poverty and evangelize and reform the world. Unfortunately, most Christians do not even tithe. So let's begin there—not 51 percent, but 10 percent.

Be Generous in Blessing the Lost

I want to encourage a lifestyle of giving, especially to those who do not know Jesus. Jesus taught in Luke 16:9 (NLT), "Here's the lesson: Use your worldly resources to benefit others and make friends. Then, when your earthly possessions are gone, they will welcome you to an eternal home."

On one occasion, I took my daughter Joy out for some daughter-daddy time. We went to a nearby restaurant. As we were finishing our meal, a group of twenty Little Leaguers with their coaches and some parents came into the restaurant, and they were seated next to our table. They were famished for lunch after playing a morning baseball game. I felt the Lord say to me, *Pick up the tab for the whole group.* I love doing this at restaurants when I see other church members, but I had never done it for a group of kids that I did not know.

I called the manager over and told him that as soon as everyone ordered to give me the bill. He was incredulous. "Are you sure you want to pick up the tab for that whole group?"

"Definitely," I answered, "but I don't want them to know it was me. But I do want you to tell them that a pastor of a nearby church paid for them."

Pastors get a bad rap for being poor and cheap and only asking for money. I wanted to break that stereotype, to show them this pastor was prospering and blessed. Not only that, I wanted to mentor my daughter in giving blessing away. As we were walking out of the restaurant, she said to me, "Dad, you are the most generous man I know!"

God wants to prosper you and bless you, too. Now decree this over your life by faith in Jesus' name:

> *I decree a blessing over my finances: I break the spirit of poverty off my life and my bloodline, and I decree that God will prosper me financially. God has blessed me with the power to gain wealth, and I decree that I will advance God's Kingdom with my generosity.*

17

Decree #10: Destiny

I decree a blessing over you to be led by His Spirit and His Word, that you will know and obey His will and that you will fulfill your prophetic destiny.

You are destined for greatness! Great are your destiny and the wonderful plans that God has for your future (Jeremiah 29:11). You are God's handiwork, created in Christ Jesus to do good works, which God prepared in advance for you to do (Ephesians 2:10). The word *handiwork* has the connotation of a skillful stroke of a master artist. Not only are you meant to display His beauty and glory, you were designed for excellent exploits. You are God's masterpiece.

The Bible instructs us to live a life worthy of this grand calling (Ephesians 4:1). I declare that you will serve the purposes of God in your generation. The cost is well worth it.

The Holy Scriptures and the Holy Spirit

Running the good race requires a steadfast commitment and obedience to His Word and the Holy Spirit. The Bible, one of the greatest gifts that have been given to humanity, "is given by inspiration of God, and is profitable for doctrine, for reproof, for correction, for instruction in righteousness, that the man [or woman] of God may be complete, thoroughly equipped for every good work" (2 Timothy 3:16). God's Word is a lamp before our feet that illuminates our paths (Psalm 119:105). I pray that you will develop a love and passion for the Scriptures. May you hide it in your heart and let the Word of Christ dwell in you richly (Colossians 3:16).

As wonderful as the Bible is, it is important not to elevate the book over whom the book is meant to reveal. Near the end of His ministry, Jesus told His disciples it was better that He leave them, for if Jesus did not ascend to heaven, the Helper (Holy Spirit) would not come to us (John 16:7). God's heart from the very beginning was to dwell with us and in us. The Holy Spirit fulfills the Lord's desire to make His tabernacle within His people (John 1:14). Through Jesus Christ, God made a way for His Spirit to literally live in us. We are now the temple of the Holy Spirit (1 Corinthians 6:19).

Unfortunately, in many faith communities the Holy Trinity could be considered "God the Father, God the Son and God the Holy Scriptures." Most believers have no issue worshiping

God or His Son, but the Holy Spirit can seem like a mysterious concept that remains nebulous. He is the Counselor who guides us into all truth (John 16:13). There is no way for us to understand the Bible or fulfill our divine call without the Holy Spirit.

Some people believe that the highest ideal in the Christian life is principle: to study the Bible and glean from it principles by which to live. I love principles, and I teach biblical principles, but principles are not enough. This is actually an inferior way of discipleship. We were first created to abide in Christ and live in the Spirit's presence. Principle without presence reduces our faith to religion, while presence elevates it to a divine relationship.

We need the Word and the Holy Spirit to fulfill our destiny. The Word and Spirit are married together, and they will never file for divorce. Bill Johnson from Bethel Church writes:

> It's hard for us to have the same fruit as the early Church when we value a book they didn't have more than we value the Holy Spirit, whom they did have. I don't say that to devalue the Bible. It is the inspired Word of God. It's just that we must reestablish the correct value for the Holy Spirit, who alone can interpret and empower us in the reading and living of the Scriptures. There is a tension between these two realities that the apostle Paul addressed when he said, *"The letter kills, but the Spirit gives life"* (2 Cor. 3:6). It's not either/or. The Spirit makes the Word come alive and enables us to live what we read.[1]

God wants you to fulfill your destiny and finish well. One of the keys to doing this is found in Jesus' quote from the Old Testament: "Man shall not live by bread alone, but by every word that proceeds from the mouth of God" (Matthew 4:4; see also Deuteronomy 8:3). The word *proceeds* is in the present tense. Living by the words of God requires maintaining a consistent, personal relationship with the Lord to know what He is currently saying. Proverbs 26:4, for example, states, "Do not answer a fool according to his folly, lest you also be like him." The very next verse instructs, "Answer a fool according to his folly, lest he be wise in his own eyes." Which command are we supposed to obey? It depends on what the Lord is saying.

Abraham's Test

Abraham was not always the father of many nations, as we know him now. He was 99 when God appeared to him and promised, "I will make you exceedingly fruitful; and I will make nations of you, and kings shall come from you" (Genesis 17:6). But Abram's wife Sarai was already 90 years old, and they did not have any children! God proclaimed that Sarai would have a son even in her old age. Their faith in God was put to the test, and God showed Himself faithful to His word. After Isaac was born, Abraham's faith was put to an even greater test. The Lord said to Abraham, "Take now your son, your only son Isaac, whom you love, and go to the land of Moriah, and offer him there as a burnt offering on one of the mountains of which I shall tell you" (Genesis 22:2).

Through his extraordinary journey, Abraham had developed a special trust with God. This new directive to sacrifice Isaac proceeded directly from the mouth of the Lord. Abraham heard and immediately responded. Early in the morning, he brought Isaac to the place of which God had told him. After building an altar and arranging the wood, he bound Isaac his son and laid him upon the wood. "And Abraham stretched out his hand and took the knife to slay his son" (Genesis 22:10). Abraham modeled true obedience through his actions. But if he had not heard the proceeding (or current) word of God, he might have killed the divine destiny that lay before him. At the last moment, the angel of the Lord called to him, saying, "Do not lay your hand on the lad, or do anything to him; for now I know that you fear God, since you have not withheld your son, your only son, from Me" (Genesis 22:12).

God's word was to sacrifice Isaac. But then God's word was not to sacrifice Isaac. To know which one was correct required Abraham to have a sensitivity and intimacy with the Lord. We were created for this type of connection to the Spirit of God. God's Word was not meant to be a religious rulebook to adhere to with zealous devotion. It was given to fill us with the Holy Spirit and draw us into the heart of God.

Living by the Spirit

We are called to live by the Spirit (Galatians 5:16). Paul says, "For as many as are led by the Spirit of God, these are sons of God" (Romans 8:14). Being led requires two basic actions: hearing what is told and obeying what is heard. Many divine instructions come through Scripture, such as love your neighbor, forgive others and give to those in need. Others come through the Holy Spirit guiding our daily lives, and we must listen to hear them. An amazing example of this is illustrated in the life of Ravi Kandal,[2] who radically encountered God at the age of seventeen and gave his life to Jesus Christ. He transformed from a teenager who wanted to kill himself into a follower of Christ committed to preaching the Gospel to the lost and untouchables of India.

Featured in Darren Wilson's film *Father of Lights*,[3] Ravi has a unique relationship with the Lord. For more than twenty years, God has woken Ravi at 4:00 every morning to speak with him in an *audible* voice!

One day, after Ravi had his usual early-morning rendezvous with Abba God, he told Darren that the Lord told him to speak to an older man with a white beard, wearing an orange robe and a turban on his head, standing next to a certain temple. They drove five hours to this temple and found the man, as the Lord had said. Ravi learned he was a guru. Not just any guru but a maharishi: a guru of gurus. It is the Hindu equivalent of an apostle.

It was risky for Ravi to speak with this religious leader because maharishis are not allowed to hear the Gospel and could incite others to stone those who try to share Jesus. But the guru listened to Ravi because he had seen Ravi in a dream! An unknown man said he needed to meet Ravi and listen to what he said. This man told him to go to that temple, and Ravi would find him. The guru traveled ten hours to get there. After meeting Ravi, he realized the unknown man was God. Sitting by a calm lake on a sunny day, Ravi led this Hindu maharishi in a prayer to accept Christ. With a smile on his face, he told Ravi about the great peace he had in his heart.

Since that encounter, the maharishi has converted his disciples and continues to tell people about Jesus. He has become an evangelist for the Kingdom and ministers with signs and wonders. All this happened because a humble child of God listened to the Holy Spirit and followed His leading.

Doing What I See the Father Do

The *way* Ravi hears from Jesus is unique; what is not unique is that Jesus is speaking to him and to you. He says, "My sheep hear My voice, and I know them, and they follow Me" (John 10:27). God is constantly speaking to us, but like Ravi, we have to cultivate a hearing heart.

People have often asked me how I came to pastor an apostolic center, lead a network of 30,000 churches and serve as chancellor of an international university. My first response is "by the grace of God." The second thing I share is that I never intended to start any of the major ministries that God has asked me to steward. He initiated all three, and I did what He asked me to do.

God woke me up at 1:00 in the morning in 1994, and I heard the words *Four, four, ninety-four*. When I heard them, I knew I was to plant a new church and the church would start on April 4, 1994. After confirmation from Sue, my family and others, HRock Church was launched. Starting HIM was also not on my horizon. I was part of the Vineyard denomination, and I thought I was going to be a Vineyard pastor for life. But in December 1995, the church and I were graciously asked to leave the Vineyard, who asked that we hold our nightly meetings outside the Vineyard covering. When I was praying about aligning with John and Carol Arnott, Cindy Jacobs called and prophesied that I was to lead my own apostolic network. The next year Harvest International Ministry was birthed. Finally, in 2010, as Peter Wagner was approaching his eightieth year, he resigned as chancellor of the Wagner Leadership Institute, and as one of his spiritual sons, I received the university from him as an inheritance.

The secret of Jesus' success is found in John 5:19: "Jesus explained, 'I tell you the truth, the Son can do nothing by himself. He does only what he sees the Father doing. Whatever the Father does, the Son also does.'" God is always successful, and He is on the move. When you join what God is doing in your life, you too will be successful. When I obey what God is showing me, I begin to fulfill my prophetic destiny.

You Are a Reformer

The book of Acts contains 28 chapters of supernatural deeds and experiences of Jesus' disciples. Interestingly, this book does not have a formal ending. The story is still being written through the Church. You are called to change the world. The same Spirit that raised Jesus from the dead is living inside of you (Romans 8:11). You plus the Holy Spirit can do the impossible.

Jesus demonstrated what one individual completely filled and led by the Spirit could accomplish. He also prophesied that not only would we do what He did, we would do even greater things (John 14:12). Receive and believe the prophetic promises over your life. He is the Good Shepherd, and His sheep know His voice, so follow Him (John 10:27). May you live the abundant life!

Make this final declaration with all your heart:

I decree a blessing over myself that I will be led by His Spirit and His Word, that I may know His ways and obey His will and that I will fulfill my prophetic destiny.

Epilogue

One Blessed Life

I want to give God glory by sharing how He has blessed my family and blessed me. After all, this book is titled *God Wants to Bless You!* I feel if I were not living the blessed life, it would be almost hypocritical for me to write it.

God has been abundantly good to me. I feel blessed beyond measure. Please know that I give Him all the praise and glory for what I write here. It is truly by *His* grace that I am what I am. I am not boasting in myself but testifying to His grace to bring you hope, encouragement and faith. If He could do all this for a former drug addict, He can surely do it in your life.

For me, success is to know God and to have a family that loves me and is happy. I am blessed to have been married to my bride and best friend for more than 35 years. Next to Jesus, Sue is the best thing in my life. She and I deeply love each other, even though we are very different from one another. That is not to say that we have not had our share of challenges in marriage, but God helped us through our "intense fellowship" times as we took our marriage covenant seriously. I share how God has blessed our marriage in one of my earlier books, *Say Goodbye to Powerless Christianity*.

I also feel blessed to have four adult children and their godly spouses. Only my youngest child, Mary, is yet to be married (but she is currently courting a young man of God, and by the time this book is published, who knows?). They all love Jesus and serve Him in some capacity. My son, Gabriel, is now a third-generation pastor, and Mary is executive director of Harvest International Ministry. My son-in-law Kuoching is the church administrator. I am also blessed to have four wonderful grandchildren, Justice, Annabelle and two more on the way.

I am blessed to lead HRock Church, the best church in the world with the best pastors and staff (of course, I am slightly biased). I lead an amazing apostolic team of phenomenal leaders through HIM. You can read about these leaders on our website, harvestim.org.

By God's grace, Sue and I have prospered financially. I do not have a financial need in the world. Not that we could not use more money—who couldn't? But God has truly met all our financial *needs* "according to His riches in glory by Christ Jesus" (Philippians 4:19). Apart from our home mortgages, we have lived debt-free through 35 years of marriage, not only from credit card debt but, by God's grace and goodness, school debt. We have paid for my and our children's college education in full, including my seminary education, four undergraduate degrees and one master's degree (Mary earned a master's in public policy at Pepperdine University—and boy, is Pepperdine expensive!). I am not saying that student loans are wrong, but we have been so blessed financially that we did not need any.

Apart from the car that the church leases for me, our cars were bought in cash. I drive a thirteen-year-old Lexus that will not die on me so I can get a new car! All of our adult children have purchased their own homes or are living in houses that we have purchased for them—and this is in L.A., one of the most expensive cities in America. Here is the best part: Since 2010, my wife and I have given more than 50 percent of whatever we earn to the Lord's work to advance His Kingdom. Yet God has prospered us financially beyond our dreams.

By God's grace, we have a physically healthy family. Sue and I are aging well. We have no disease, pain or sickness; at our last annual checkup we received a clean bill of health. In fact, by God's grace I have not even had the flu or been in bed with a fever in years. The world will say, "Knock on wood," or "Don't press your luck," but I do not believe in luck. I believe we are blessed by God and that it is God's will for His children to enjoy good health (3 John 2). I have not missed a speaking engagement or one Sunday of preaching because of sickness. I have walked in divine health. Again, I say that "this was the LORD's doing; it is marvelous in our eyes" (Psalm 118:23).

Paul said, "Let him who boasts, boast in the Lord" (1 Corinthians 1:31 NASB). Do you think God loves me more than He loves you? Of course not! He is perfect in love and shows no partiality. Are God's blessings for a select few? No, they are for all who *believe*—that is the key word. The source of all blessing is ours because of what Jesus did on the cross two thousand years ago (Galatians 3:13).

The Bible makes an incredible statement in Ephesians 1:3: "Blessed be the God and Father of our Lord Jesus Christ, who has blessed us with every spiritual blessing in the heavenly places in Christ." God has already given to every believer every blessing in the heavenly realms; it is our job to pull it down to earth by faith.

God wants you to live a blessed life as a testimony to the world, with confidence that this will lead others to Christ. I believe this will be one of the greatest evangelistic methods God will use to bring in the end-time harvest. God's blessing will be used to bless all families of the world, bringing nations to know and worship Jesus as the one and only true God!

Notes

Introduction

1. Brennan Manning, *The Signature of Jesus* (Colorado Springs: Multnomah, 1996), 149–50.

Chapter 1: The Blessing Hunger

1. "Statistics," *The Fatherless Generation* (blog), http://thefatherless generation.wordpress.com/statistics/.

2. C. S. Lewis, *Mere Christianity* (San Francisco: HarperCollins, 1952), 136–137.

Chapter 2: What Does Blessing Look Like?

1. Ben Carson, *Gifted Hands* (Grand Rapids, Mich.: Zondervan, 1990), 11–221.

Chapter 3: God Is Good

1. A. W. Tozer, *The Knowledge of the Holy* (New York: HarperCollins, 1961), 1.

2. Baylor Institute for Studies of Religion, "American Piety in the 21st Century" (Baylor Religion Survey, Baylor University, Waco, Tex., September 2006), 26–30, http://www.baylor.edu/content/services/document.php/33304.pdf.

3. W. E. Vine, *Vine's Complete Expository Dictionary of Old and New Testament Words* (Nashville: Thomas Nelson, 1996), 142.

Chapter 4: God's Blessings on Israel

1. Luana Goriss, "Jewish Nobel Prize Winners," December 3, 2014, http ://judaism.about.com/od/culture/a/nobel.htm.

2. Steven Silbiger, *The Jewish Phenomenon* (Atlanta: Longstreet Press, 2000), 4.

3. Joel Stein, "Who Runs Hollywood? C'mon," *Los Angeles Times*, December 19, 2008.

Chapter 5: The Great Exchange of the Cross

1. Billy Graham, *Peace with God* (Nashville: Thomas Nelson, 2000), 71.

2. Ibid., 78.

3. The Hebrew word translated "infirmities" or "pain" is *choliy*, which, according to *Strong's Concordance*, means malady, anxiety or calamity. In other places it is translated "disease" or "sickness" (as in Deuteronomy 7:15).

4. This Hebrew word is *mak'ob*, which means anguish or affliction. In Jeremiah 51:8 it is translated "pain."

5. Ché Ahn, *The Grace of Giving* (Minneapolis: Chosen, 2013), 137. (Originally published Ventura, Calif.: Regal, 2013.)

6. Matthew Henry, *Commentary of the Whole Bible* (Grand Rapids, Mich.: Zondervan, 1961), 1834.

7. Ahn, *Giving*, 160–61.

8. More details on how God delivered me from the spirits of mammon and poverty can be found in *The Grace of Giving* (Chosen, 2013).

Chapter 7: The Power of Decrees

1. Leon Morris, *The Gospel According to Matthew* (Grand Rapids, Mich.: Eerdmans Publishing, 1992), 426.

2. C. Peter Wagner, *Apostles and Prophets: The Foundation of the Church* (Minneapolis: Chosen, 2000), 25. (Originally published Ventura, Calif.: Regal, 2000.)

3. Kurtis Lee, Jordan Steffen, and Ryan Parker, "Firefighters Make Progress Against Black Forest Fire," *The Denver Post*, June 14, 2013.

Chapter 8: Decree #1: Love

1. Jennifer Thompson, interview by Dick Gordon, *The Story*, American Public Media, June 13, 2013, http://www.thestory.org/stories/2013-06/jennifer -thompson.

Chapter 9: Decree #2: The Grace of God

1. C. Peter Wagner, *Humility* (Grand Rapids, Mich.: Chosen, 2002), 18–19, 81–82.

Chapter 10: Decree #3: The Power of the Holy Spirit

1. Ché Ahn, *Spirit-Led Evangelism* (Grand Rapids, Mich.: Chosen, 2006), 134–135. Adapted. Used by permission.

2. Grand Rapids, Mich.: Chosen, 2012.

3. Kevin Dedmon, *Unlocking Heaven* (Shippensburg, Pa.: Destiny Image, 2009), 79.

Chapter 12: Decree #5: Christlike Character

1. Colin Brown, ed., *Dictionary of New Testament Theology* (Grand Rapids, Mich.: Zondervan, 1976), 538–539.

2. Ibid., 539.

3. Ibid.

4. Ibid., 544.

Chapter 14: Decree #7: Healing and Blessing

1. I captured her testimony on my iPhone on April 26, 2013.

2. W. E. Vine, *An Expository Dictionary of New Testament Words* (Old Tappan, N.J.: Revell, 1966), 280.

3. Stephen More and Julian L. Simon, *It's Getting Better All the Time* (Washington, D.C.: Cato Institute, 2000), Kindle edition, loc584.

4. Ibid., loc660.

5. The full testimony can be seen on YouTube.com, under the name "Amazing Healing Testimony from VOA 2014!"

Chapter 15: Decree #8: Family

1. The Pew Research Center, "Section 1: A Demographic Portrait of Muslim Americans," in *Muslim Americans: No Signs of Growth in Alienation or Support for Extremism* (Washington, D.C.: Pew Research Center, 2011), http ://www.people-press.org/files/legacy-pdf/Muslim%20American%20Report %2010-02-12%20fix.pdf.

2. Ché Ahn, *How to Pray for Healing* (Minneapolis: Chosen, 2003), 58–59. (Originally published Ventura, Calif.: Regal, 2003.)

3. Get specifics for evangelizing your family members in my book *Spirit-Led Evangelism* (Chosen, 2006).

Chapter 16: Decree #9: Prosperity

1. Peter Wagner, *The Great Transfer of Wealth* (New Kensington, Pa.: Whitaker House, 2015), 44.

Chapter 17: Decree #10: Destiny

1. Bill Johnson, "Going from Glory to Glory," in *The Reformer's Pledge*, comp. Ché Ahn (Shippensburg, Pa.: Destiny Image, 2010), 91.

2. You can learn more about Ravi at his website, www.kingdomfoundations .org.

3. *Father of Lights*, directed by Darren Wilson (Elgin, Ill.: Wanderlust Productions, 2012), DVD.

Ché Ahn and his wife, Sue, have been the founding pastors of HRock Church in Pasadena since 1994. Ché is the founder and president of Harvest International Ministry, a worldwide apostolic network of churches in more than sixty nations with the common vision of "changing lives, transforming cities, and discipling nations." He is also chancellor of the Wagner Leadership Institute, an international network of apostolic training centers established to equip the saints for Kingdom ministry.

Ché received his master of divinity and doctor of ministry from Fuller Theological Seminary and has played a key role in many strategic local, national and international outreaches, including serving as president of TheCall, a youth prayer movement. He has authored numerous books, including *Say Goodbye to Powerless Christianity*, *How to Pray for Healing* and *The Grace of Giving*. He ministers extensively throughout the world, bringing apostolic wisdom with a Holy Spirit impartation of revival, healing and evangelism. His greatest desire is to see society transformed through Christians who understand and fulfill their ordained purposes.

Ché and Sue have been married for more than 35 years. They have four adult children and four grandchildren.

For more information about Ché Ahn, his ministries and his resource materials, visit www.hrockchurch.com, www.harvestim.org and www.wagnerleadership.org.

More from Ché Ahn

For more information about his ministry, go to cheahn.org.

God desires to prosper His people, and He will do so as we trust His grace to provide for our needs and seek to reflect His giving nature. But in order to flourish in God's provision, we must repent of the hindrances of mind and heart that lead us to grasp at wealth in unhealthy ways.

The Grace of Giving

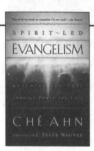

Evangelism is not an assignment. It is a privilege—an overflow of God's life in you that brings more life in return, both to you and to others. This practical guide will transform your thinking, ignite your heart for the lost and show you how simple and natural personal evangelism can be.

Spirit-Led Evangelism

✔Chosen